W9-BQH-150

greatvegetarianfood

greatvegetarianfood

The Australian Women's Weekly
cookbook

contents

vegetarian vitals

The most important thing a vegetarian should know is that variety is not only the spice of life but also the way to health. Research into vegetarian diets has shown that as long as you eat a wide variety of food, you should have no problem obtaining all the nutrients you need. This means eating foods from four main groups every day: cereals and grains; pulses, nuts and seeds; fruits and vegetables; and soy and/or dairy products. When you consider the large range of dishes that can be made from these groups you can see the benefits of a vegetarian life.

So, what sorts of foods fit into these four main food groups? Some examples of cereals and grains are barley, buckwheat, maize, millet, oats, rye, wheat and rice. Pulses, nuts and seeds include dried or canned beans and peas, lentils, almonds, cashews, peanuts, pistachios, walnuts, sunflower seeds, sesame seeds and pumpkin seeds. The fruit and vegetable category includes dried fruit. Soy and/or dairy products range from milks to cheese, yogurt and tofu.

A healthy alternative

Cooking healthy meals for vegetarians is no more difficult than cooking for those who eat meat, it just takes a little getting used to. The recent trend towards simple, seasonal cooking, and an increasing concern for good health, has broadened the appeal of vegetarian food; these days you would be hard-pressed to find a restaurant or cafe without at least one vegetarian dish on the menu. And the enormous influence that other countries have had on our eating habits in recent years has helped ensure vegetarian meals are never dull. In fact, many of the best recipes originate in countries where vegetarian cuisine is the norm.

A vegetarian diet is relatively inexpensive, which is one of the reasons it's so appealing to young people. Added to that, plant-based foods are loaded with nutrients, including protein, iron and calcium, and contain no saturated (or "bad") fats. In short, a varied vegetarian diet is healthy and satisfying.

A well-balanced vegetarian meal

There is a huge range of dishes to choose from: it could be spicy bean casserole (page 215), served with sourdough toast; char-grilled salad with polenta rounds and pesto (page 68); potato and herb pie (page 80); penne primavera (page 109); tacos with kidney beans (page 191), or you could go for a more casual meal of steamed rice paper parcels (page 25). Just try to make sure it's varied and balanced – vegetables by themselves are not enough.

The nuts and bolts of nutrition

To make sure you maintain a healthy diet, it helps to know the basics of nutrition – which vitamins and minerals you may need to keep an eye on, and where to find them. It is not necessary to become a nutrition mastermind – just keep meals varied and the rest will take care of itself. Following is a brief rundown.

iron

Iron is necessary for the formation of blood, and also for growth in children, the maintenance of a healthy immune system, and energy production. There is often concern that a plant-based diet is deficient in iron, as red meat is its most recognised source and contains the type of iron most easily absorbed. However, there are many sources of iron other than red meat and studies have shown its absorption can be enhanced by eating vitamin C-rich foods at the same time. On the other hand, tannins (found in tea and coffee) and calcium from dairy products can inhibit iron absorption, so avoid these when eating iron-rich meals. Using cast-iron cookware when cooking also contributes to dietary intake. A lack of iron in the diet can result in anaemia.

good sources of iron for vegetarians include:

breakfast cereals fortified with iron; pumpkin, sesame and sunflower seeds; most types of nuts; peanut butter; lentils, chickpeas and hummus; soy beans; tofu; soy flour; red kidney beans and other beans (including baked beans); wheat bran, wheatgerm and wholemeal flour; quinoa; dried figs, raisins, apricots, peaches and prunes; and black treacle.

symptoms of anaemia:

pallor, fatigue and lethargy, breathlessness upon exertion, dizziness, palpitations, insomnia, headaches and poor concentration.

supplements

iron supplements should only be taken if recommended by a doctor – pregnant women are often advised to take low-dose iron supplements.

calcium

Calcium is essential for healthy bones and teeth, as well as nerve and muscle function, and blood clotting. Those who avoid dairy products run the risk of calcium deficiency and should regularly eat other foods that are high in calcium. Interestingly, there's no evidence of calcium deficiency among vegans (who don't eat dairy products). This is possibly because they keep an eye on their calcium intake, or it may be that those on plant-based diets (which are low in protein) may actually need less calcium than flesh eaters, whose diet is high in protein.

good sources of calcium for vegetarians include:

milk and calcium-enriched soy milk, cheese, yogurt, leafy green vegetables (especially broccoli), figs, sesame seeds and tahini.

osteoporosis

This condition, in which bones become brittle due to a lack of calcium, is better prevented than treated, so a diet that provides adequate calcium is important from an early age. Post-menopausal women, who produce less oestrogen, are more susceptible and should be getting from 1000-1500mg of calcium per day. Middle-aged men need 800-1000mg per day.

protein

Proteins are made up of amino acids, and are necessary for cell growth and maintaining tissues, and to help protect the body against infection. For a while it was thought that proteins needed to be combined to make them "complete" (in terms of amino acids), however vegetarian diets have been found to naturally supply the recommended amounts of all the indispensable amino acids. So, as long as your diet is varied and your energy needs are met, you should have no problem getting all the protein your body needs. In fact, flesh eaters are often found to consume far more protein than they need, which is believed to put them at greater risk of health problems such as heart disease, strokes and various cancers.

good sources of protein for vegetarians include:
grains and cereals, tofu, peanut butter, nuts, baked beans, eggs, yogurt, milk, pasta, seeds and pulses (peas, beans and lentils).

fats

Everyone needs a little fat in their diet, but it's important to know the difference between saturated and unsaturated fat, and as much as possible, to eat unsaturated. Most saturated fat comes from animals: butter, cream, etc. But some vegetable oils, palm oil, for example, are also partly saturated. Read labels and go for polyunsaturated fats (nuts, grains and seeds) and monounsaturated fats (olive oil, avocados). Polyunsaturated fats known as omega-3 and omega-6 are thought to protect the body from heart disease.

good sources of fatty acids for vegetarians include:
Omega 6 fatty acids are found in sesame, safflower and sunflower oils.
Omega 3 fatty acids are found in linseed oil, canola oil, olive oil, nut oils (such as macadamia, almond and walnut) and leafy green vegetables.

carbohydrates

fibre and

Fibre keeps the body regular and carbohydrates are our most important source of energy. Plant foods are loaded with fibre and carbohydrates, so a vegetarian diet is more than sufficient in both these areas.

good sources of fibre for vegetarians include:
cereals, whole-grain products, dried and fresh beans and peas, spinach, dried and fresh fruits and potatoes.

good sources of carbohydrates for vegetarians include:
breads, pasta, grains, potatoes, pulses and bananas.

vine-ripened tomatoes

vitamins

A varied, healthy vegetarian diet provides most vitamins easily, except perhaps vitamin B2 (riboflavin) and vitamin B12. A vegetarian should not have to take vitamin supplements to be healthy, but if you're worried about your vitamin intake, check with your doctor.

good sources of vitamins for vegetarians include:

Vitamin B2 found in milk, cheese, yogurt, almonds, cashews, pine nuts, pecans, seeds, dried apricots and prunes, quinoa, millet, wheatgerm, barley, molasses, snow peas and mushrooms.

Vitamin B12 found in dairy foods and eggs, as well as products fortified with vitamin B12, such as breakfast cereals and some soy milks.

Vitamin A found in red, orange and yellow vegetables, as well as leafy green vegetables, peaches, apricots, eggs, milk and cheese.

Vitamin C found in fresh fruit (citrus fruit especially), salad leaves, leafy green vegetables, blackcurrants, tomatoes and potatoes.

Vitamin D made in the body when it is exposed to sunlight. It is also found in milk and butter.

Vitamin E found in vegetable oils, whole-grain cereals, eggs, soy beans and avocados.

ss brown mushrooms

pregnancy

Your nutrient and energy needs are increased by about 10 per cent when you become pregnant. If you can, it's a good idea to improve your diet several months before becoming pregnant, eating especially more folic acid (found in dark-green leafy vegetables), whole grains (like brown rice), wholewheat bread and pulses. You need more calcium and iron during pregnancy too (see page 7 for sources).

breastfeeding

It can be hard to maintain a healthy diet during breastfeeding, when there seems to be no time to do anything for yourself. However, breastfeeding women do require extra nutrients and energy (about 20 per cent more than usual). Look to pulses, whole grains (like brown rice), and especially nuts, seeds and dried fruits, which are easy to nibble on throughout the day.

teenagers

Growing bodies need lots of energy, so foods that are rich in carbohydrates, such as breads, pasta, potatoes, grains and pulses, are perfect. Girls also need to keep up their iron and calcium levels – if there is any doubt, a doctor can determine if these are sufficient.

fine print

hidden animal products

Animal fats such as lard, which can be found in pastry products. Always check labels and look for foods that contain unsaturated vegetable fats instead.

Animal rennet (made from the lining of a calf's stomach) is sometimes used to make cheese. Look for cheeses that were made using vegetable rennet – this will be specified on the packet.

Gelatine (made from animal bones and hooves) is often used in savoury and sweet products as a setting agent.

Sauces and stocks always check the labels carefully as many have animal-based ingredients.

Ready-made meals always read the labels carefully before choosing to ensure that no animal-based ingredients have been used.

Alcohol many alcoholic drinks, such as wines and beers, are "fined" (clarified) using animal ingredients.

Note: We have used some prepared products that may contain animal-based ingredients, such as prepared curry pastes which may contain shrimp paste. We were unable to find substitutes that wouldn't compromise the flavour of the dish. Omit them if you wish.

hit list

Variety is all-important. Try different foods and different cooking methods regularly.

Use fruit and vegetables **as soon as possible** after buying, so they are at their freshest. Their flavour will be better, and they won't have lost nutrients in deterioration.

Steam vegetables rather than boiling them to keep as many nutrients as possible.

Eat whole, unrefined foods often and sweetened, fatty refined foods rarely.

When frying foods, **use vegetable oils** or a non-stick pan.

Choose **low-fat versions of dairy foods** where possible.

Buy **whole-grain products** if possible, such as wholegrain bread, as major vitamins and minerals can be reduced during processing.

Breakfast really is the most important meal of the day, and fortified breakfast cereals are a great way to supplement a diet with minerals and vitamins.

corn and pea
samosas

1½ cups (225g) plain flour

30g ghee

1 tablespoon cumin seeds

½ cup (125ml) warm water, approximately

vegetable oil, for deep-frying

filling

10g ghee

½ small brown onion (40g), chopped finely

1 clove garlic, crushed

1 teaspoon grated fresh ginger

1 teaspoon cumin seeds

1 teaspoon coriander seeds

2 teaspoons garam masala

¼ teaspoon ground turmeric

¼ teaspoon chilli powder

⅔ cup (110g) drained canned corn kernels

⅔ cup (130g) frozen peas, thawed

¼ cup (60ml) coconut cream

1 Place flour in medium bowl; rub in ghee. Add seeds; gradually stir in enough of the water to mix to a firm dough. Knead on lightly floured surface about 5 minutes or until smooth. Cover; refrigerate 30 minutes. While pastry is chilling, prepare filling.

2 Roll pastry on lightly floured surface until 2mm thick. Cut pastry into 8cm rounds.

3 Place level teaspoons of the filling into centre of each round; brush edges of pastry with water. Press edges together using thumb and finger; repeat with remaining pastry and filling. *[Can be made 1 day ahead to this stage and refrigerated, covered.]*

4 Heat oil in medium frying pan; deep-fry samosas, in batches, until browned lightly and cooked through.

filling Heat ghee in medium saucepan. Cook onion, garlic, ginger, seeds and spices; stir over low heat until onion is soft. Add corn, peas and coconut cream; bring to a boil. Remove from heat; cool to room temperature.

makes 30

per samosa 3.3g fat; 263kJ
store Recipe can be frozen up to 4 months.

finger food

Mini pappadums with curried egg, and cucumber and
kumara sushi are just a couple of delicious pre-meal
appetisers that are surprisingly simple to prepare.

broad bean and ricotta
dip

PREPARATION TIME 25 MINUTES (plus refrigeration time) ■ COOKING TIME 5 MINUTES

500g fresh or frozen broad beans

1¼ cups (250g) ricotta cheese

2 tablespoons lemon juice

1 clove garlic, crushed

**1 tablespoon finely chopped
    fresh parsley**

1 Boil, steam or microwave broad beans until soft; cool. Remove and discard skins.

2 Blend or process beans with remaining ingredients until smooth; spoon into serving dish. Cover; refrigerate 1 hour before serving.

3 Serve dip with crudités if desired.

makes 2 cups (500ml)

per tablespoon 1.3g fat; 91kJ

store Recipe n be made 1 day ahead and refrigerated, covered.

cucumber and kumara
sushi

PREPARATION TIME 35 MINUTES (plus refrigeration time) ▓ COOKING TIME 15 MINUTES (plus standing time)

vegan

1 cup (200g) short-grain rice

**1 lebanese cucumber
(130g), seeded**

½ cup (125ml) rice wine vinegar

2 teaspoons sesame oil

400g kumara, chopped finely

4 sheets nori (seaweed)

2 tablespoons white sesame seeds

1 Place rice in large saucepan of boiling water. Reduce heat; simmer, covered, about 15 minutes or until tender, stirring occasionally. Drain; stand until cool.

2 Cut cucumber into matchstick-size pieces; combine with vinegar and oil in small bowl. Stand 1 hour; drain.

3 Boil, steam or microwave kumara until tender; drain. Mash to give a smooth puree.

4 Using wet fingers press a quarter of the rice on plastic-wrap-lined-bamboo sushi mat. Place one nori sheet over rice, rough-side up. Spread a quarter of the kumara over nori; sprinkle with a quarter of the sesame seeds. On narrow side closest to you, arrange a quarter of the cucumber. Using narrow side of mat closest to you, start rolling sushi; press firmly as you roll. Repeat process with remaining ingredients to make a total of four rolls. Cover; refrigerate 1 hour before cutting.

5 Cut each roll into six pieces.

makes 24

per serving 3.1g fat; 663kJ
store Sushi can be made 1 day ahead and refrigerated, covered.

mini pappadums
with curried egg

PREPARATION TIME 15 MINUTES

3 hard-boiled eggs, shelled
1 tablespoon mayonnaise
1 tablespoon mango chutney
1 teaspoon mild curry paste
1 green onion, chopped finely
2 teaspoons finely chopped fresh coriander
75g packet ready to eat mini pappadums
3 red thai chillies, sliced thinly
2 green onions, extra, sliced thinly

1 Mash eggs in small bowl with mayonnaise, chutney and curry paste until combined. Stir in onion and coriander. *[Can be made 1 day ahead to this stage and refrigerated, covered.]*

2 Just before serving, top pappadums with rounded teaspoons of egg mixture.

3 Top with chilli and extra onion.

makes 20

per serving 1.3g fat; 122kJ
store Curried egg mixture can be made 1 day ahead and refrigerated, covered.
tip Regular pappadums can be substituted for ready-to-eat mini pappadums, if preferred. Break into quarters; shallow-fry.

cheese
fillo triangles

PREPARATION TIME 40 MINUTES ■ COOKING TIME 15 MINUTES

150g fetta cheese, crumbled

125g ricotta cheese

1 egg, beaten lightly

pinch of nutmeg

freshly ground pepper

12 sheets fillo pastry

100g butter, melted

1 Combine cheeses, egg, nutmeg and pepper in small bowl. *[To prevent pastry sheets drying out, cover with damp tea-towel until you are ready to use them.]* Brush two pastry sheets with a little of the butter; place one pastry sheet on top of the other. Cut layered sheets into four strips lengthways.

2 Place 2 teaspoons of the cheese mixture at one end of each strip. Fold one corner end of the pastry diagonally across filling to other edge, forming a triangle. Continue folding to the end of strip, retaining the shape. Brush triangles with a little more of the butter. Repeat with remaining pastry, filling and butter. *[Can be made 3 hours ahead to this stage and refrigerated, covered.]*

3 Place triangles on greased oven trays; bake, uncovered, in moderately hot oven about 15 minutes or until browned.

makes 24

per serving 5.8g fat; 327kJ
store Recipe can be frozen up to 4 months.

fetta dip

PREPARATION TIME 10 MINUTES

200g fetta cheese
3/4 cup (150g) ricotta cheese
2 tablespoons lemon juice
2 tablespoons olive oil
1 clove garlic, quartered

1 Crumble fetta into large bowl; stir in remaining ingredients. Process mixture, in batches, until smooth.

2 Serve with bruschetta, if desired.

makes 1 3/4 cups (385g)

per tablespoon 4.8g fat; 225kJ
store Dip can be made 2 days ahead and refrigerated, covered.
tip Stir leftover dip through mashed potatoes, add 1 tablespoon of either finely chopped fresh oregano or mint to dip, if desired.

beetroot dip

PREPARATION TIME 10 MINUTES ■ COOKING TIME 45 MINUTES

3 medium beetroot (500g), trimmed
1 clove garlic, crushed
200g yogurt
1 teaspoon ground cumin
2 teaspoons lemon juice

1 Cook beetroot in large saucepan of boiling water, uncovered, about 45 minutes or until tender. Drain; cool 5 minutes. Wearing gloves, peel beetroot while warm; chop coarsely.

2 Blend or process beetroot with garlic, yogurt, cumin and juice until smooth.

3 Serve with toasted shards of pitta, if desired.

makes 2 cups (585g)

per tablespoon 0.3g fat; 63kJ
store Dip can be made 1 day ahead and refrigerated, covered.

caramelised onion and tomato tart

PREPARATION TIME 10 MINUTES ■ COOKING TIME 35 MINUTES

vegan
26cm frozen pizza base
6 small ripe tomatoes (780g), halved
2 medium red onions (340g), sliced thinly
2 cloves garlic, crushed
1/4 cup fresh rosemary
2 tablespoons tomato paste
1 teaspoon rock salt

1 Cut six 8cm rounds from pizza base. Place tomato in large ovenproof dish or tray; bake, uncovered, in very hot oven about 20 minutes or until softened.

2 Meanwhile, cook onion, garlic and two-thirds of the rosemary in large, oiled, heavy-base saucepan, stirring occasionally, about 20 minutes or until onion is caramelised. *[Can be made 1 day ahead to this stage and refrigerated, covered.]*

3 Spread pizza base rounds with paste; top with onion mixture and tomato. Sprinkle with salt and remaining rosemary.

4 Bake, uncovered, in hot oven about 15 minutes or until browned and heated through.

serves 6

per serving 1.7g fat; 729kJ

eggplant dip

PREPARATION TIME 20 MINUTES ■ COOKING TIME 1 HOUR

vegan

1 large eggplant (500g)
2 cloves garlic, crushed
1 tablespoon white wine vinegar
1/4 cup (60ml) olive oil
1/4 cup finely chopped fresh flat-leaf parsley

1 Place whole eggplant on oven tray; pierce in a few places using fork. Bake, uncovered, in hot oven about 1 hour or until soft.

2 Remove eggplant from oven; cool slightly. Remove and discard skin; chop flesh coarsely. Place flesh in sieve; press out excess juice.

3 Mash eggplant flesh in medium bowl using fork. Stir in remaining ingredients.

4 Serve with vienna bread, pickled chillies and olives, if desired.

serves 8

per serving 7g fat; 303kJ
store Dip can be made 2 days ahead and refrigerated, covered.

yogurt and cucumber dip

PREPARATION TIME 2 HOURS 10 MINUTES

500g Greek-style yogurt or plain yogurt
1 lebanese cucumber (130g), peeled, grated coarsely
1/2 teaspoon salt
1 clove garlic, crushed
1 tablespoon lemon juice
1 1/2 tablespoons shredded fresh mint

1 Place yogurt onto large square of double-thickness muslin cloth. Tie ends of cloth together; hang over large bowl, or place in sieve. Refrigerate for about two hours or until the yogurt is thick.

2 Meanwhile, combine cucumber and salt in small bowl; stand 20 minutes. Gently squeeze out excess liquid.

3 Combine yogurt, cucumber, garlic, juice and a tablespoon of the mint in small bowl; mix well. Serve topped with remaining mint.

serves 8

per serving 2.2g fat; 203kJ
store Dip can be made 1 day ahead and refrigerated, covered.

dolmades

PREPARATION TIME 50 MINUTES ■ COOKING TIME 1 HOUR 40 MINUTES

vegan

1/4 cup (60ml) olive oil

1 medium (170g) red onion, chopped finely

6 green onions, sliced thinly

2 cloves garlic, crushed

1 teaspoon ground cumin

1 teaspoon grated lemon rind

1 cup (200g) long-grain white rice

1.5 litres (6 cups) water

1/4 cup finely chopped fresh parsley

1/4 cup finely chopped fresh mint

48 vine leaves in brine (250g)

1/2 cup (125ml) lemon juice

1 Heat 1 tablespoon of the oil in medium saucepan; cook onions, garlic, cumin and rind, stirring, until onions are tender.

2 Add rice and 2 cups of the water; cook, stirring, about 5 minutes or until water is absorbed. Cool slightly; stir in parsley and mint.

3 Drain vine leaves; wash under cold water. Pat dry with absorbent paper. Place two vine leaves, overlapping slightly, on bench. Place rounded tablespoons of rice mixture in centre of each pair of leaves; roll tightly to enclose. Repeat with remaining mixture and leaves.

4 Place dolmades, overlapped edges underneath, close together, in large saucepan. Pour combined remaining oil, remaining water and juice over dolmades. Place medium plate on top to keep dolmades in position while cooking. Cover pan with foil; bring to a boil. Reduce heat; simmer, covered, about 1 1/2 hours or until dolmades are cooked through.

5 Non-vegans can serve dolmades with yogurt, if desired.

makes 24

per dolmade 2.5g fat; 236kJ
store Dolmades can be made 2 days ahead and refrigerated, covered.

chilli cornbread
muffins

PREPARATION TIME 10 MINUTES ■ COOKING TIME 15 MINUTES

1 tablespoon olive oil
4 green onions, chopped finely
1/4 cup finely chopped fresh coriander
1/2 small red capsicum (75g), chopped finely
1 clove garlic, crushed
2 red thai chillies, chopped finely
1/2 teaspoon ground cumin
1 cup (170g) polenta
1/2 cup (75g) self-raising flour
1/2 teaspoon bicarbonate of soda
1 egg
1/2 cup (125ml) buttermilk
60g butter, melted

coriander cream
3/4 cup (180ml) light sour cream
1/2 teaspoon sambal oelek
1 tablespoon finely chopped fresh coriander
1 green onion, chopped finely

1 Heat oil in medium saucepan; cook onion, coriander, capsicum, garlic, chilli and cumin, stirring, until capsicum is soft. Transfer to large bowl.

2 Stir in polenta, flour and soda; stir in combined remaining ingredients. Spoon mixture into three greased 12 hole (1 tablespoon) mini muffin pans.

3 Bake, uncovered, in moderately hot oven about 10 minutes or until browned.

4 Turn muffins onto wire racks to cool; serve with coriander cream.

coriander cream Combine ingredients in small bowl.
[Can be made 1 day ahead and refrigerated, covered.]

makes 36

per serving 3.2g fat; 232kJ
store Muffins can be frozen up to 6 months.

ginger gow gees
with chilli lime sauce

PREPARATION TIME 1 HOUR ■ COOKING TIME 30 MINUTES

(vegan) **cooking-oil spray**

1 small red capsicum (150g), chopped finely

1 small kumara (250g), grated

1 small bok choy (150g), chopped finely

2 green onions, chopped finely

2 teaspoons grated fresh ginger

1 clove garlic, crushed

1 cup (80g) bean sprouts, chopped finely

1 tablespoon finely chopped fresh mint

40 gow gee wrappers

chilli lime sauce

1 tablespoon low-salt soy sauce

2 teaspoons lime juice

2 teaspoons sugar

¼ teaspoon sambal oelek

1 Coat medium non-stick saucepan with cooking-oil spray; cook capsicum, kumara, bok choy, onion, ginger and garlic, stirring, until vegetables are just tender. Stir in sprouts and mint.

2 Place rounded teaspoons of capsicum mixture on centre of each wrapper; brush edges with water. Gather together in centre; press firmly to seal. *[Can be made 3 hours ahead to this stage and refrigerated, covered.]*

3 Place gow gees in single layer in baking-paper-lined steamer; cook, covered, over simmering water about 20 minutes or until cooked through. Serve with chilli lime sauce.

chilli lime sauce Combine ingredients in small bowl; mix well. *[Can be made 1 day ahead and refrigerated, covered.]*

makes 40

per gow gee 0.2g fat; 99kJ

steamed rice paper
parcels

PREPARATION TIME 30 MINUTES (plus standing time) ▪ COOKING TIME 5 MINUTES

vegan

2 dried shiitake mushrooms
150g firm tofu
8 round rice paper sheets
150g baby bok choy, shredded finely
1 green onion, chopped finely
1 tablespoon bottled fried onion

soy dipping sauce
1 tablespoon light soy sauce
1 teaspoon chinese rice wine
1/2 teaspoon sambal oelek
1/2 teaspoon sesame oil

1 Place mushrooms in small heatproof bowl; cover with boiling water. Stand 20 minutes; drain. Discard stems; slice caps thinly. Slice tofu into eight slices; combine with 2 teaspoons of the soy dipping sauce in medium bowl.

2 Place each rice paper sheet, individually, into medium bowl of warm water about 1 minute or until softened slightly; lift gently from water. Place on board; pat dry with absorbent paper. Top each sheet with one slice of tofu, an eighth of the bok choy, green onion and mushrooms. Fold rice paper over vegetables; fold in sides. Fold over to make a parcel.

3 Place parcels, tofu-side up, in single layer, in baking-paper-lined steamer; cook, covered, over simmering water about 5 minutes or until heated through. Serve accompanied by remaining dipping sauce and bottled fried onion.

soy dipping sauce Combine ingredients in small bowl.

makes 8

per serving 1.8g fat; 201kJ

puff pastry cheese straws

PREPARATION TIME 15 MINUTES
COOKING TIME 12 MINUTES

2 sheets ready-rolled puff pastry

1 egg, beaten lightly

½ cup (40g) finely grated parmesan cheese

1 Brush pastry sheets with egg; sprinkle one sheet with cheese. Top with other pastry sheet; press together.

2 Cut into 1.5cm strips; cut each strip in half. Twist strips; place about 2cm apart on greased oven trays.

3 Bake, uncovered, in moderately hot oven about 12 minutes or until strips are browned lightly.

makes 30

per serving 3.1g fat; 207kJ
store Straws can be made 1 week ahead and stored in an airtight container.

bagel chips

PREPARATION TIME 10 MINUTES
COOKING TIME 15 MINUTES (plus cooling time)

4 bagels

3 teaspoons peanut oil

2 cloves garlic, crushed

½ teaspoon dried oregano

1 Using serrated or electric knife, cut bagels into very thin slices. Place slices in single layer on oven trays; brush lightly on one side of each slice with combined oil, garlic and oregano.

2 Bake, uncovered, in moderately slow oven about 15 minutes or until browned lightly; cool chips on trays.

makes 40

per serving 5.3g fat; 1481kJ
store Bagel chips can be made 1 month ahead and stored in an airtight container.

potato skins

PREPARATION TIME 15 MINUTES
COOKING TIME 1 HOUR 20 MINUTES

vegan

8 medium old potatoes (1.6kg)

2 tablespoons olive oil

**1 tablespoon finely chopped
fresh rosemary**

2 teaspoons salt

1 teaspoon cracked black pepper

1 Place unpeeled potatoes on oven tray. Bake, uncovered, in moderate oven about 1 hour or until tender; cool.

2 Cut each potato into six wedges; scoop out flesh, leaving skins intact. Reserve potato flesh for another use.

3 Place potato skins in single layer on wire rack over oven tray. Brush with oil; sprinkle with combined rosemary, salt and pepper. Bake, uncovered, in hot oven about 20 minutes or until crisp.

makes 48

per serving 0.8g fat; 42kJ
tip Potato skins can be served hot or at room temperature; use scooped out flesh in potato salad or bubble and squeak.

cajun pitta crisps

PREPARATION TIME 10 MINUTES
COOKING TIME 10 MINUTES

vegan

5 large pitta pocket breads

¼ cup (60ml) olive oil

1 tablespoon cajun seasoning

1 Split each pitta bread in half; cut each half into quarters. Place bread in single layer on oven trays. Brush with oil; sprinkle with seasoning.

2 Bake, uncovered, in moderately hot oven about 10 minutes or until browned and crisp.

makes 40

per serving 1.6g fat; 158kJ
store Pitta crisps can be made 1 week ahead and stored in an airtight container.

dippers

spicy corn chowder
with tortilla crisps

PREPARATION TIME 35 MINUTES ■ COOKING TIME 1 HOUR 20 MINUTES

6 medium corn cobs (1.5kg)

2 tablespoons vegetable oil

2 medium brown onions (300g), chopped finely

2 trimmed sticks celery (150g), chopped finely

4 cloves garlic, crushed

2 teaspoons sambal oelek

1 tablespoon sweet paprika

2 teaspoons cumin seeds

2 large potatoes (600g), chopped finely

1 litre (4 cups) vegetable stock

1 cup (250ml) cream

capsicum and parsley puree

3 large red capsicums (1kg)

2 tablespoons finely chopped fresh parsley

½ cup (125ml) sour cream

tortilla crisps

3 packaged flour tortillas

vegetable oil, for deep-frying

1 Cut corn kernels from cobs. Heat oil in large saucepan; cook onion, celery, garlic, sambal oelek and spices, stirring, until onion is soft.

2 Stir in corn, potato and stock; simmer, covered, 1 hour. Add cream; stir until heated through.

3 Top with capsicum and parsley puree; serve with tortilla crisps.

capsicum and parsley puree Quarter capsicums; remove and discard seeds and membranes. Roast under grill or in very hot oven, skin-side up, until skin blisters and blackens. Cover capsicum pieces in plastic or paper for 5 minutes; peel away skin. Blend or process capsicum, parsley and cream until smooth.

tortilla crisps Cut each tortilla into 12 triangles. Heat oil in large frying pan. Deep-fry tortilla pieces, in batches, until browned lightly and crisp; drain on absorbent paper.

serves 6

per serving 38.8g fat; 2934kJ

store Chowder and puree can be made 1 day ahead and refrigerated, covered, separately; tortilla crisps can be made 1 week ahead and stored in an airtight container.

soups

Hearty vegetable soups have always been a favourite
and our roasted pumpkin kumara soup and spicy
corn chowder with tortilla crisps are no exception.

broad bean
and corn soup

PREPARATION TIME 25 MINUTES ■ COOKING TIME 35 MINUTES

vegan

1.5kg broad beans, shelled
6 fresh corn cobs (2.5kg)
1 large carrot (180g)
1 tablespoon peanut oil
1½ tablespoons grated ginger
3 cloves garlic, crushed
2 litres (8 cups) vegetable stock
1½ tablespoons soy sauce
2 green onions, sliced thinly
½ cup (40g) bean sprouts

1 Boil, steam or microwave beans until just soft; drain. Refresh under cold water; remove and discard skin from beans.

2 Cut corn kernels from cobs; cut carrot into matchstick-size pieces.

3 Heat oil in large saucepan; cook ginger and garlic, stirring, 1 minute. Add stock and sauce; bring to a boil. Add beans, corn and carrot; cook, uncovered, about 5 minutes or until corn is tender.

4 Just before serving, stir onion and sprouts into soup.

serves 6

per serving 6.5g fat; 1499kJ

tip 500g packet frozen broad beans can be substituted for fresh beans, if preferred.

roasted pumpkin
kumara soup

PREPARATION TIME 25 MINUTES ▨ COOKING TIME 55 MINUTES

vegan

2 large brown onions (400g)

750g jap pumpkin,
  cut into 5cm cubes

1 large kumara (500g),
  cut into 5cm cubes

2 large carrots (360g),
  cut into 2cm slices

4 cloves garlic, peeled

2 teaspoons cumin seeds

1 teaspoon coriander seeds

olive oil spray

3 cups (750ml) vegetable stock

⅓ cup fresh coriander leaves

1 Peel onions and cut into eight wedges.

2 Combine vegetables in large baking dish with garlic and seeds; coat with olive oil spray.

3 Bake, uncovered, turning occasionally, about 40 minutes or until vegetables are tender and golden brown.

4 Puree vegetables with stock, in batches, in food processor or blender until smooth; strain into large saucepan. Cover; bring to a boil. Serve topped with coriander leaves.

serves 4

per serving 3g fat; 1087kJ
store Soup can be made 2 days ahead and refrigerated, covered, or frozen up to 6 months.

hearty minestrone
with cheesy garlic bread

PREPARATION TIME 30 MINUTES ▓ COOKING TIME 1 HOUR 10 MINUTES

1 tablespoon olive oil

1 medium white onion (150g), sliced thickly

1 medium carrot (120g), chopped coarsely

1 medium leek (350g), sliced thickly

2 small potatoes (240g), chopped coarsely

100g green beans, halved

2 trimmed sticks celery (150g), chopped coarsely

2 cloves garlic, crushed

1.5 litres (6 cups) vegetable stock

400g can tomatoes

2 tablespoons tomato paste

3/4 cup (135g) macaroni

2 small zucchini (180g), chopped coarsely

cheesy garlic bread

8 thick slices italian-style bread (150g)

1/4 cup (60ml) olive oil

2 cloves garlic, crushed

1/2 cup (60g) finely grated cheddar cheese

1 Heat oil in large saucepan; cook onion, carrot, leek, potato, beans, celery and garlic, stirring, until onion is soft.

2 Add stock, undrained crushed tomatoes and paste; bring to a boil. Reduce heat; simmer, covered, stirring occasionally, about 45 minutes or until vegetables are tender.

3 Add pasta and zucchini; boil, uncovered, about 10 minutes or until pasta is tender. *[Can be made 1 day ahead to this stage and refrigerated, covered.]*

4 Serve minestrone with cheesy garlic bread.

cheesy garlic bread Brush one side of the bread slices with combined oil and garlic; grill or toast on both sides until browned lightly. Sprinkle with cheese; grill until cheese melts.

serves 4

per serving 26.9g fat; 2444kJ

store Minestrone can be frozen up to 3 months.

tip Make two batches at once and freeze in single serves for easy meals.

gazpacho

PREPARATION TIME 30 MINUTES (plus refrigeration time)

vegan

1 litre (4 cups) tomato juice

10 medium egg tomatoes (750g), chopped coarsely

2 medium red onions (340g), chopped coarsely

2 cloves garlic, quartered

1 lebanese cucumber (130g), chopped coarsely

2 tablespoons sherry vinegar

1 medium red capsicum (200g), chopped coarsely

1 small red onion (100g), chopped finely, extra

1 lebanese cucumber (130g), chopped finely, extra

1 small red capsicum (150g), chopped finely, extra

1 tablespoon finely chopped fresh dill

1 Blend or process juice, tomato, onion, garlic, cucumber, vinegar and capsicum, in batches, until pureed. Cover; refrigerate 3 hours. *[Can be made 1 day ahead to this stage and refrigerated, covered.]*

2 Just before serving, divide soup among serving bowls; stir equal amounts of extra onion, extra cucumber, extra capsicum and dill into each bowl.

serves 6

per serving 0.4g fat; 366kJ

store Gazpacho can be frozen, without extra vegetables, up to 3 months.

tip Add a finely chopped red chilli to juice mixture, while blending, to make a spicier gazpacho.

leek soup
with parmesan potato dumplings

PREPARATION TIME 30 MINUTES ■ COOKING TIME 55 MINUTES

50g butter

1 medium brown onion (150g),
   chopped coarsely

2 cloves garlic, quartered

3 large leeks (1.5kg), sliced thinly

2 large potatoes (600g),
   chopped coarsely

3 cups (750ml) vegetable stock

1.5 litres (6 cups) water

½ cup (125ml) cream

1 tablespoon finely chopped fresh
   garlic chives

parmesan potato dumplings

2 medium potatoes (400g),
   chopped coarsely

20g butter

2 tablespoons sour cream

¼ cup (20g) finely grated
   parmesan cheese

2 tablespoons finely chopped fresh
   garlic chives

1 cup (150g) self-raising flour

1 egg, beaten lightly

1 Melt butter in large saucepan; cook onion, garlic and leek, stirring, until leek softens.

2 Add potato, stock and the water; bring to a boil. Reduce heat; simmer, covered, 25 minutes.

3 Blend or process soup mixture, in batches, until smooth. *[Can be made 1 day ahead and refrigerated, covered.]*

4 Return soup to cleaned pan; stir over heat until hot. Drop rounded tablespoons of dumpling mixture into soup; simmer, uncovered, about 10 minutes or until dumplings are cooked through, stirring occasionally to turn dumplings. Stir in cream and chives.

parmesan potato dumplings Boil, steam or microwave potato until tender; drain. Mash potato, butter and sour cream in medium bowl until smooth. Add remaining ingredients; mix well.

serves 6

per serving 24.3g fat; 1976kJ

pumpkin dhal soup
with pumpkin coriander scones

PREPARATION TIME 20 MINUTES (plus standing time) ■ COOKING TIME 1 HOUR

1 cup (200g) yellow split peas (toor dhal)
1 tablespoon vegetable oil
2 medium brown onions (300g), chopped finely
1 tablespoon ground turmeric
1 tablespoon ground cumin
1 tablespoon ground coriander
1 tablespoon yellow mustard seeds
1 tablespoon grated fresh ginger
1 litre (4 cups) vegetable stock
1.3kg pumpkin
1 litre (4 cups) water
1 tablespoon vegetable oil, extra
1 teaspoon ground nutmeg

pumpkin coriander scones
2 cups (300g) self-raising flour
1/4 cup finely chopped fresh coriander
3/4 cup (180ml) buttermilk, approximately

1 Cover split peas with water; stand, covered, 2 hours or overnight.

2 Drain split peas. Rinse under cold water; drain.

3 Heat oil in large saucepan; cook onion, stirring, until soft. Add turmeric, cumin, coriander, seeds and ginger; cook, stirring, until fragrant. Stir in stock and split peas; bring to a boil. Reduce heat; simmer, uncovered, 10 minutes.

4 Meanwhile, finely grate enough of the pumpkin to make 3 cups; coarsely chop remaining pumpkin. Add the water and half of the grated pumpkin to mixture in pan; reserve remaining grated pumpkin for pumpkin coriander scones. Simmer, uncovered, about 30 minutes or until soup thickens. [Can be made 1 day ahead to this stage and refrigerated, covered.]

5 Combine chopped pumpkin and extra oil in baking dish; sprinkle with nutmeg. Bake, uncovered, in moderately hot oven about 20 minutes or until browned and tender.

6 Serve topped with roasted pumpkin, accompanied by pumpkin coriander scones.

pumpkin coriander scones Grease 20cm round sandwich pan. Place flour in large bowl; stir in coriander and reserved pumpkin. Stir in enough of the buttermilk to mix to a soft, sticky dough; knead dough on floured surface about 5 minutes or until smooth and elastic. Press dough to 3cm thickness; cut into 5cm rounds. Place scones in prepared pan; bake, uncovered, in hot oven about 25 minutes or until scones sound hollow when tapped. Turn onto wire rack to cool.

serves 6

per serving 10.2g fat; 1914kJ
store Soup and scones can be frozen, separately, up to 3 months.

zuppa
primavera

PREPARATION TIME 25 MINUTES ■ COOKING TIME 35 MINUTES

2 tablespoons olive oil

1 medium leek (350g), sliced thinly

2 cloves garlic, crushed

1 tablespoon plain flour

3 cups (750ml) vegetable stock

1.5 litres (6 cups) water

100g squash, chopped coarsely

150g farfalle pasta

**500g fresh asparagus,
   cut into 2cm lengths**

100g snow peas, halved

100g sugar snap peas, halved

1 cup (250ml) cream

3 green onions, sliced diagonally

1 Heat oil in large saucepan; cook leek and garlic, stirring, about 5 minutes or until leek softens. Add flour; cook, stirring, until mixture bubbles and thickens. Gradually stir in stock; cook, stirring, until mixture boils and thickens slightly.

2 Add the water, squash and pasta; cook, uncovered, about 10 minutes or until squash and pasta are just tender.

3 Stir in asparagus and peas; cook, uncovered, about 5 minutes or until asparagus is just tender.

4 Just before serving, add cream and onion; stir soup over heat until hot.

serves 6

per serving 28.5g fat; 1662kJ

tip Test pasta and squash occasionally to ensure neither overcooks.

tomato
and borlotti bean soup

PREPARATION TIME 15 MINUTES ■ COOKING TIME 25 MINUTES

vegan

2 medium brown onions (300g), chopped coarsely

2 cloves garlic, crushed

11 large egg tomatoes (1kg), chopped coarsely

2 cups (500ml) vegetable stock

1 tablespoon worcestershire sauce

2 tablespoons finely chopped fresh parsley

2 x 400g cans borlotti beans, rinsed, drained

1 Heat oiled large saucepan; cook onion and garlic, uncovered, stirring, until onion softens.

2 Stir in tomato; cook, stirring, about 3 minutes or until tomato softens.

3 Add stock and sauce; bring to a boil. Reduce heat; simmer, covered, 15 minutes. Blend or process tomato mixture, in batches, until almost smooth.

4 Return tomato mixture to pan. Stir in parsley and beans; simmer, uncovered, about 5 minutes or until hot.

serves 4

per serving 0.8g fat; 417kJ

store Recipe can be made 2 days ahead and refrigerated, covered, or frozen up to 6 months.

lime and chilli **laksa**

PREPARATION TIME 30 MINUTES ■ COOKING TIME 40 MINUTES

You will need 100g fresh coriander for this recipe.

2 tablespoons peanut oil

3¼ cups (800ml) coconut milk

1 litre (4 cups) vegetable stock

¼ cup (60ml) lime juice

1 tablespoon palm sugar

10 kaffir lime leaves, torn

600g fried tofu, chopped coarsely

500g baby bok choy, trimmed, quartered

375g rice stick noodles

2 cups (160g) bean sprouts

1 lebanese cucumber (130g), seeded, sliced thinly

2 green onions, sliced thinly

2 tablespoons fresh coriander leaves

2 tablespoons fresh vietnamese mint

laksa paste

1 tablespoon shrimp paste

¼ cup (36g) grated fresh galangal

3 large red thai chillies, chopped coarsely

1 tablespoon ground coriander

2 teaspoons ground cumin

1 teaspoon ground turmeric

1 medium brown onion (150g), chopped coarsely

3 cloves garlic, quartered

⅓ cup coarsely chopped coriander roots and stems

¼ cup coarsely chopped fresh lemon grass

1 Heat oil in large saucepan; cook laksa paste, stirring, until fragrant. Add coconut milk, stock, juice, sugar and lime leaves; bring to a boil. Reduce heat; simmer, uncovered, 25 minutes. Stir tofu and bok choy into laksa mixture.

2 Meanwhile, place noodles in large heatproof bowl; cover with boiling water. Stand until just tender; drain. Divide noodles among serving bowls; top with laksa mixture. Sprinkle with sprouts, cucumber, onion, coriander and mint.

3 Serve accompanied by sambal oelek and wedges of lime, if desired.

laksa paste Blend or process ingredients until mixture forms a smooth paste.

serves 4

per serving 74.5g fat; 4701kJ

tip Shrimp paste can be omitted from laksa paste for vegans.

carrot and lentil soup
with caraway toast

PREPARATION TIME 25 MINUTES ▪ COOKING TIME 55 MINUTES

**1.125 litres (4½ cups)
vegetable stock**

**2 large brown onions (400g),
chopped finely**

4 cloves garlic, crushed

1 tablespoon ground cumin

**6 large carrots (1kg),
chopped coarsely**

**2 trimmed sticks celery (150g),
chopped coarsely**

2 cups (500ml) water

½ cup (100g) brown lentils

½ cup (125ml) buttermilk

caraway toast

8 slices (200g) ciabatta bread

**⅓ cup (25g) finely grated
parmesan cheese**

1 teaspoon caraway seeds

**2 tablespoons finely chopped
fresh parsley**

1 Heat ½ cup (125ml) stock in large saucepan; cook onion, half of the garlic and cumin, stirring, until onion softens. Add carrot and celery; cook, stirring, 5 minutes.

2 Add remaining stock and the water; bring to a boil. Reduce heat; simmer, uncovered, about 20 minutes or until carrot softens.

3 Blend or process soup, in batches, until smooth; return soup to pan. Add lentils; simmer, uncovered, about 20 minutes or until lentils are tender. [Can be made 1 day ahead to this stage and refrigerated, covered.]

4 Stir buttermilk into hot soup; serve with caraway toast.

caraway toast Place ciabatta, in single layer, on oven tray; toast under hot grill until browned. Sprinkle combined cheese, remaining garlic, seeds and parsley over untoasted sides of ciabatta. Grill until topping is browned lightly and cheese melts; cut in half.

serves 4

per serving 4.5g fat; 1433kJ

tomato
and bread soup

PREPARATION TIME 30 MINUTES ■ COOKING TIME 45 MINUTES

vegan

**100g piece ciabatta bread,
cut into 2cm slices**

1 tablespoon olive oil

**2 large brown onions (400g),
chopped finely**

3 cloves garlic, crushed

**2kg tomatoes, peeled,
chopped coarsely**

2 litres (8 cups) vegetable stock

2 tablespoons tomato paste

1 teaspoon sugar

**¼ cup loosely packed, coarsely
chopped fresh basil**

1 Place bread on oven tray; bake, uncovered, in hot oven about 10 minutes or until crisp. *[Can be made 2 days ahead to this stage and stored in an airtight container.]*

2 Heat oil in large saucepan; cook onion and garlic, stirring, until onion is soft. Add tomato; cook, stirring occasionally, about 10 minutes or until tomato is pulpy.

3 Break bread into large pieces directly into pan. Add stock, paste and sugar; simmer, uncovered, about 15 minutes or until soup thickens slightly. Stir occasionally to break up any bread pieces. Just before serving, stir in basil.

4 Drizzle with extra virgin olive oil, if desired.

serves 6

per serving 4.3g fat; 862kJ

tip Any leftover stale bread having a hard, crunchy crust can be substituted for ciabatta, if unavailable.

rosemary damper

PREPARATION TIME 20 MINUTES
COOKING TIME 45 MINUTES

60g butter

**1 medium brown onion (150g),
chopped finely**

3 cups (450g) self-raising flour

**2 tablespoons finely chopped
fresh rosemary**

1 cup (125g) grated tasty cheese

1¼ cups (310ml) water, approximately

1 Melt 15g of the butter in small frying pan.
Cook onion, stirring over medium heat about
2 minutes or until onion is soft; cool.

2 Sift flour into large bowl; rub in remaining butter.
Stir in onion mixture, rosemary and 2/3 cup of
the cheese; make well in centre. Stir in enough
of the water to mix to a soft dough; knead on
lightly floured surface until smooth.

3 Place dough onto greased oven tray; pat
into 16cm circle. Using sharp knife, cut 1cm
deep cross in top of dough. Brush with a
little extra milk; sprinkle with remaining cheese.

4 Bake, uncovered, in moderate oven about
40 minutes or until damper is golden brown
and sounds hollow when tapped.

makes 1 loaf
per loaf 97g fat; 10494kJ
store Damper can be made 3 hours ahead and stored at
room temperature, or frozen up to 2 months.

corn bread

PREPARATION TIME 25 MINUTES (plus standing time)
COOKING TIME 20 MINUTES

2 teaspoons (7g) dried yeast

½ cup (125ml) warm water

½ cup (125ml) warm milk

2 cups (300g) plain flour

½ cup (85g) polenta

½ teaspoon salt

2 teaspoons polenta, extra

1 Mix yeast with the water in small bowl; stir in milk.
Sift flour into large bowl; stir in polenta and salt.
Stir in yeast mixture; mix to a firm dough. Knead
dough on floured surface about 10 minutes or
until dough is smooth and elastic; place dough in
greased large bowl. Cover; stand in warm place
about 1 hour or until doubled in size.

2 Turn dough onto floured surface; knead further
5 minutes. Shape dough into 13cm round; place
on lightly greased oven tray. Using sharp knife,
cut 1cm deep cross into top of dough. Stand,
covered, in warm place 20 minutes; sprinkle with
extra polenta.

3 Bake, uncovered, in moderately hot oven
about 20 minutes or until bread sounds hollow
when tapped.

makes 1 loaf
per loaf 10.7g fat; 1017kJ
store Corn bread can be made 3 hours ahead and stored at
room temperature.

beer bread

PREPARATION TIME 20 MINUTES
COOKING TIME 50 MINUTES

3¼ cups (485g) self-raising flour
2 teaspoons salt
2 teaspoons sugar
375ml bottle light beer

1 Grease 14cm x 21cm loaf pan; line bases with baking paper.

2 Sift flour, salt and sugar into medium bowl; make well in centre. Pour in beer all at once; using spoon, mix to a soft, sticky dough.

3 Knead dough on floured surface until smooth; divide in half. Knead each half; place in prepared pan.

4 Bake, uncovered, in moderate oven about 50 minutes or until bread is browned and sounds hollow when tapped. Turn onto wire rack; serve warm or cold.

makes 1 loaf
per loaf 5.8g fat; 7132kJ
store Beer bread can be made 3 hours ahead and stored at room temperature.

irish soda bread

PREPARATION TIME 10 MINUTES
COOKING TIME 50 MINUTES

2⅔ cups (420g) wholemeal plain flour
2½ cups (375g) white plain flour
1 teaspoon salt
1 teaspoon bicarbonate of soda
**2¾ cups (680ml)
    buttermilk, approximately**

1 Sift flours, salt and soda into large bowl; return husks from sieve to bowl. Stir in enough of the buttermilk to mix to a firm dough.

2 Knead dough on floured surface until just smooth. Shape dough into 20cm round; place on greased oven tray.

3 Using sharp knife, cut 1cm-deep cross into top of dough. Bake, uncovered, in moderate oven about 50 minutes. Lift onto wire rack to cool.

makes 1 loaf
per loaf 27.5g fat; 12746kJ

dampers

grilled salad
with creamy dressing

PREPARATION TIME 35 MINUTES (plus standing time) ▧ COOKING TIME 30 MINUTES

2 medium potatoes (400g), peeled

1 large kumara (500g), peeled

200g medium flat mushrooms

cooking-oil spray

1 teaspoon cajun seasoning

250g spinach, trimmed

1 green oak leaf lettuce

creamy dressing

¼ cup (15g) sun-dried tomatoes without oil

½ cup (125ml) low-fat milk

½ cup (125ml) light sour cream

2 teaspoons finely chopped fresh oregano

1 clove garlic, crushed

2 teaspoons balsamic vinegar

1 Boil, steam or microwave potato and kumara until just tender; pat dry with absorbent paper. Cut potato and kumara into 1cm-thick slices.

2 Coat potato, kumara and mushrooms with cooking-oil spray; sprinkle with seasoning. Cook, in batches, on heated oiled grill plate (or grill or barbecue) until vegetables are browned and tender.

3 Serve with torn spinach and lettuce leaves; drizzle with creamy dressing.

creamy dressing Cover tomatoes with boiling water in small heatproof bowl; stand about 20 minutes or until soft. Drain tomatoes; chop finely. Whisk milk and sour cream in small bowl. Stir in tomato, oregano and garlic; whisk in vinegar.

serves 4

per serving 6.7g fat; 1030kJ

starters and salads

Begin each meal with a light, healthy combination of greens in these salads or other tasty creations, such as asparagus with citrus-toasted breadcrumbs and potato salad with olives and macadamias.

warm haloumi
and spinach salad

PREPARATION TIME 15 MINUTES ■ COOKING TIME 15 MINUTES

400g haloumi cheese, sliced thickly

150g baby spinach leaves

100g mixed lettuce leaves

300g can chickpeas, rinsed, drained

280g char-grilled eggplant, drained, sliced thickly

560g char-grilled capsicum, drained, sliced thickly

warm tomato dressing

2 teaspoons olive oil

1 small red onion (100g), chopped finely

1 clove garlic, crushed

1⅓ cups (330ml) tomato juice

½ teaspoon sugar

1 teaspoon balsamic vinegar

1 tablespoon finely chopped fresh basil

1 Heat oiled large saucepan; cook cheese until browned both sides.

2 Layer ingredients on serving platter or plates.

3 Just before serving, drizzle salad with warm tomato dressing.

   warm tomato dressing Heat oil in small saucepan; cook onion and garlic, stirring, until onion is soft. Add juice, sugar and vinegar; stir until hot. Blend or process tomato mixture until smooth; stir in basil.

serves 6

per serving 18.7g fat; 1268kJ

zucchini flowers
filled with suppli rice

PREPARATION TIME 20 MINUTES ■ COOKING TIME 45 MINUTES

2 teaspoons olive oil

1 small brown onion (80g),
    chopped finely

1 clove garlic, crushed

½ cup (100g) arborio rice

¼ cup (60ml) dry white wine

1½ cups (375ml) vegetable stock

¼ cup (20g) finely grated
    parmesan cheese

50g fetta cheese, chopped coarsely

18 fresh zucchini flowers (250g)

150g baby spinach leaves

⅓ cup loosely packed fresh
    basil leaves

⅓ cup loosely packed fresh
    flat-leaf parsley

1 tablespoon balsamic vinegar

2 tablespoons olive oil, extra

⅔ cup (50g) shaved
    parmesan cheese

1 Heat oil in medium saucepan; cook onion and garlic, stirring, until onion is soft. Add rice, wine and stock; bring to a boil. Reduce heat; simmer, uncovered, stirring occasionally, about 12 minutes or until rice is tender and liquid is absorbed. Stir in grated parmesan and fetta; cool.

2 Remove and discard stamens from centre of zucchini flowers. Fill flowers with rice mixture; twist petal tops to enclose filling. Place filled flowers on oiled oven tray; bake, uncovered, in very hot oven about 15 minutes or until browned lightly and heated through.

3 Meanwhile, combine spinach, basil and parsley in medium bowl; toss with combined vinegar and extra oil.

4 Serve zucchini flowers with spinach salad; sprinkle with shaved parmesan.

serves 6

per serving 12.4g fat; 902kJ
tip Mozzarella or fontina cheese can be substituted for fetta cheese, if preferred.

potato salad
with olives and macadamias

PREPARATION TIME 20 MINUTES ■ COOKING TIME 20 MINUTES

(vegan)

500g baby new potatoes
1 tablespoon white wine vinegar
2 teaspoons olive oil
1/4 cup finely chopped chives
15g seeded ligurian olives
1 tablespoon toasted, coarsely chopped macadamias
1 mignonette lettuce
80g watercress, trimmed

1 Cook potatoes in large saucepan of boiling water about 10 minutes or until tender; drain.

2 Peel potatoes; combine in large bowl with vinegar, oil, chives, olives and nuts.

3 Arrange lettuce on serving plates; top with potato salad and watercress.

serves 4

per serving 7.2g fat; 662kJ

gado gado in lettuce cups

PREPARATION TIME 15 MINUTES

vegan

¼ **small chinese cabbage (200g), shredded**

¼ **cup firmly packed fresh coriander leaves**

1 **cup (80g) bean sprouts**

2 **green onions, sliced thinly**

1 **telegraph cucumber (400g), chopped coarsely**

100g **firm tofu, chopped coarsely**

8 **iceberg lettuce leaves**

peanut dressing

½ **cup (125ml) coconut milk**

⅓ **cup (50g) finely chopped roasted peanuts**

1 **tablespoon finely grated fresh ginger**

2 **teaspoons finely grated lime rind**

1 **small red thai chilli, seeded, chopped finely**

1 **tablespoon soy sauce**

1 Combine cabbage, coriander, sprouts, onion, cucumber, tofu and peanut dressing in large bowl; mix gently.

2 Serve gado gado in lettuce leaves.

peanut dressing Combine ingredients in medium bowl; mix well.
[Can be made 1 day ahead and refrigerated, covered.]

serves 4

per serving 15g fat; 860kJ

asparagus
with citrus-toasted breadcrumbs

PREPARATION TIME 15 MINUTES ■ COOKING TIME 10 MINUTES

40g butter

2 tablespoons peanut oil

1½ cups (105g) stale breadcrumbs

**2 tablespoons finely grated
orange rind**

2 cloves garlic, crushed

750g asparagus, trimmed

8 sprigs fresh tarragon

**1 cup (80g) shaved
parmesan cheese**

1 Heat half of the butter and oil in wok or large frying pan. Stir-fry combined breadcrumbs and rind until browned lightly; remove from wok.

2 Heat remaining butter and oil in wok; stir-fry garlic and asparagus, in batches, until asparagus is tender.

3 Serve asparagus with tarragon, breadcrumbs and cheese.

serves 6

per serving 16.6g fat; 1019kJ

greek salad

PREPARATION TIME 10 MINUTES

6 medium egg tomatoes (450g), chopped coarsely

3 lebanese cucumbers (400g), chopped coarsely

1 medium green capsicum (200g), chopped coarsely

1 small red onion (100g), cut into thin wedges

1 cup (150g) kalamata olives

1 teaspoon sea salt

1/2 cup (125ml) extra virgin olive oil

150g piece fetta cheese

1/2 teaspoon crushed dried rigani

1 Combine tomato, cucumber, capsicum, onion and olives in large serving bowl. Add salt and almost all of the oil; toss gently. *[Can be made 3 hours ahead to this stage and refrigerated, covered.]*

2 Cut cheese into two large pieces; place on top of salad. Sprinkle cheese with rigani; drizzle with remaining oil.

serves 8

per serving 18.9g fat; 896kJ

tip Oregano can be substituted for dried rigani, if unavailable.

mixed mushrooms
in garlic butter

PREPARATION TIME 20 MINUTES ■ COOKING TIME 20 MINUTES

2 tablespoons peanut oil

1 large brown onion (200g),
   sliced thinly

2 cloves garlic, crushed

400g cap mushrooms, quartered

400g swiss brown mushrooms

400g button mushrooms

2 teaspoons garlic salt

100g butter, chopped coarsely

1 Heat oil in wok or large frying pan; stir-fry onion, garlic and mushrooms, in batches, until tender.

2 Return mushrooms to wok with garlic salt and butter; stir-fry until butter melts.

3 Serve on toast, sprinkled with baby basil leaves, if desired.

serves 4

per serving 30.3g fat; 1397kJ

potato and onion tarts

PREPARATION TIME 30 MINUTES (plus refrigeration time) ■ COOKING TIME 30 MINUTES (plus cooling time)

¾ cup (110g) plain flour

30g reduced-fat margarine

25g butter

**1 tablespoon iced
water, approximately**

**9 medium egg tomatoes
(675g), halved**

**1 medium brown onion (150g),
sliced thinly**

1 teaspoon brown sugar

1 teaspoon balsamic vinegar

**1 large potato (300g),
peeled, quartered**

½ cup (125ml) hot skim milk

**⅓ cup (40g) grated reduced-fat
cheddar cheese**

1 Place flour in small bowl; rub in combined margarine and butter until mixture resembles coarse breadcrumbs. Add just enough of the water to form a soft dough; knead dough lightly, on floured surface, until smooth. Cover; refrigerate 30 minutes or until firm.

2 Place tomato, cut-side up, in large ovenproof dish; bake, uncovered, in hot oven about 10 minutes or until browned lightly and soft.

3 Cook onion in heated oiled small saucepan until soft. Add sugar and vinegar; cook, stirring, about 5 minutes or until onion is caramelised.

4 Boil, steam or microwave potato until tender; drain. Mash potato in medium bowl. Add milk, cheese, and onion mixture; stir until combined.

5 Roll pastry between sheets of baking paper until large enough to line six 12cm loose-bottom flan tins. Lift pastry into tins and press into sides; trim edges. Place tins on oven tray; cover pastry with dried beans or rice. Bake, uncovered, in moderately hot oven about 10 minutes; remove paper and beans. Bake, uncovered, further 10 minutes or until browned lightly; cool pastry cases. *[Pastry cases can be made 1 day ahead and stored in an airtight container.]*

6 Divide potato mixture between flan tins; bake about 10 minutes or until browned lightly. Remove tarts from flan tins; top with roasted tomatoes. Drizzle with olive oil, if desired.

serves 6

per serving 7.4g fat; 836kJ
store Pastry cases can be frozen up to 6 months.

eggplant
and salsa fresca

vegan PREPARATION TIME 30 MINUTES ■ COOKING TIME 25 MINUTES

10 baby eggplants (600g)
2 tablespoons peanut oil
1 medium white onion (150g), sliced thinly
2 cloves garlic, crushed
1 teaspoon sambal oelek
1 cup (250ml) tomato juice
6 green onions, sliced thinly

salsa fresca
1 lebanese cucumber (130g)
1 large tomato (250g), seeded, chopped finely
1 trimmed stick celery (75g), chopped finely
¼ teaspoon Tabasco sauce
1 tablespoon lime juice

1 Halve eggplants lengthways; cut four long strips through each piece lengthways, stopping about 1cm from stem end.

2 Heat half of the oil in wok or large frying pan; stir-fry eggplant, in batches, until just browned.

3 Heat remaining oil in wok; stir-fry white onion, garlic and sambal oelek. Return eggplant to wok with juice; stir-fry until eggplant is tender.

4 Serve eggplant mixture topped with salsa fresca and green onion.

salsa fresca Halve cucumber lengthways; remove and discard seeds. Chop flesh in small dice; combine cucumber in small bowl with remaining ingredients. *[Can be made 3 hours ahead and refrigerated, covered.]*

SERVES 4

per serving 10g fat; 757kJ

mesclun salad
with tarragon dressing

PREPARATION TIME 10 MINUTES

vegan **150g mesclun**

tarragon dressing
¹/₃ cup (80ml) olive oil
1¹/₂ tablespoons tarragon vinegar
1 teaspoon seeded mustard
1 clove garlic, crushed
¹/₄ teaspoon sugar

1 Wash and dry mesclun; place in serving bowl. *[Can be made 8 hours ahead to this stage and refrigerated, covered.]*

2 Just before serving, add enough tarragon dressing to lightly coat leaves; toss gently.

tarragon dressing Combine ingredients in screw-top jar; shake well. *[Can be made 1 day ahead to this stage and refrigerated, covered.]*

serves 6

per serving 12.2g fat; 471kJ

beetroot and cucumber
salad

PREPARATION TIME 20 MINUTES ■ COOKING TIME 20 MINUTES (plus cooling time)

vegan

1kg baby beetroot, trimmed

1 telegraph cucumber (400g), halved, seeded, sliced thickly

6 green onions, sliced thickly

3 trimmed sticks celery (225g), sliced thickly

dressing

2 tablespoons extra light olive oil

¼ cup (60ml) lemon juice

1 clove garlic, crushed

1 tablespoon finely chopped fresh oregano

1 teaspoon sugar

1 Place beetroot in oiled baking dish; bake, uncovered, in hot oven about 20 minutes or until tender. Cool slightly; peel. *[Can be made 1 day ahead to this stage and refrigerated, covered.]*

2 Combine beetroot, cucumber, onion and celery in large bowl; drizzle with dressing.

dressing Combine ingredients in screw-top jar; shake well.

serves 6

per serving 6.6g fat; 463kJ

roasted capsicums

vegan

PREPARATION TIME 10 MINUTES
COOKING TIME 5 MINUTES (plus standing time)

4 medium yellow capsicums (800g)

4 medium red capsicums (800g)

½ cup (125ml) olive oil

3 cloves garlic, sliced thinly

2 tablespoons finely chopped
   fresh parsley

skewers

1 Quarter capsicums; remove seeds and membranes. Roast capsicum under grill or in very hot oven, skin-side up, until skin blisters and blackens. Cover with plastic or paper 5 minutes. Peel away skin; cut capsicum into thick strips.

2 Combine capsicum with remaining ingredients in medium bowl; thread onto skewers.

serves 10

per serving 11.6g fat; 544kJ

store Roasted capsicums can be made 3 days ahead and refrigerated, covered.

marinated mushrooms

vegan

PREPARATION TIME 15 MINUTES
COOKING TIME 5 MINUTES

1 litre (4 cups) white vinegar

2 cups (500ml) water

2 teaspoons salt

800g button mushrooms

1 tablespoon fresh thyme leaves

1 clove garlic, sliced finely

1½ cups (375ml) hot olive
   oil, approximately

1 Heat vinegar, the water and salt in medium non-reactive pan until hot; do not boil. Add mushrooms; simmer gently, uncovered, 5 minutes. Drain; discard vinegar mixture.

2 Combine hot mushrooms, thyme and garlic in large heatproof bowl; mix well. Pour oil over mushroom mixture, taking care as it will bubble.

3 Place mushroom mixture in hot sterilised jar. Add oil; ensure mushrooms are covered completely. Leave 1cm space between mushrooms and top of jar; seal jar.

serves 8

per serving 21.6g fat; 906kJ

store Mushrooms can be made 3 months ahead and refrigerated.

oven-dried tomatoes

vegan PREPARATION TIME 25 MINUTES
COOKING TIME 8½ HOURS

25 medium egg tomatoes (2kg)
½ cup loosely packed fresh basil leaves
3 medium fresh red dutch chillies (10g)
3 cloves garlic, sliced thinly
1 tablespoon sea salt
olive oil

1 Cut tomatoes in half lengthways. Place basil, chillies, garlic and tomato, cut-side up, on wire racks over oven trays.

2 Sprinkle tomato with salt. Bake, uncovered, in very slow oven until basil, chillies, garlic and tomato are dry. Turn and rearrange tomato frequently while drying. *[Basil and garlic will take about 45 minutes to dry, chillies about 2½ hours, and tomato about 8½ hours.]*

3 Pack tomato, basil, chillies and garlic into hot, sterilised jars. Add oil; ensure tomato is covered completely. Leave 1cm space between tomato and top of jars; seal jars.

serves 10

per serving 13.9g fat; 633kJ
store Tomatoes can be made 6 months ahead and refrigerated.

marinated olives

vegan PREPARATION TIME 10 MINUTES (plus marinating time)

250g green olives
250g kalamata olives
2 lime wedges
2 cups (500ml) olive oil
1 clove garlic, sliced thinly
⅓ cup (80ml) lime juice
6 sprigs fresh thyme, halved
3 sprigs fresh rosemary

1 Combine ingredients in large hot sterilised jar; ensure olives are covered in oil. Leave 1cm space between oil and top of jar; seal jar.

serves 8

per serving 22.4g fat; 1011kJ
store Olives are best made at least 2 weeks before serving and stored in a cool dark place.

antipasto

baked ricotta
with char-grilled vegetables

PREPARATION TIME 20 MINUTES ■ COOKING TIME 1 HOUR

4 cups (800g) ricotta cheese

3 eggs, beaten lightly

2 tablespoons olive oil

½ teaspoon dried chilli flakes

char-grilled vegetables

1 large red capsicum (350g), sliced thickly

1 large green capsicum (350g), sliced thickly

1 large eggplant (500g), sliced thickly

3 large zucchini (450g), sliced thickly

4 small egg tomatoes (240g), cut into wedges

2 medium lemons (280g), quartered

3 small red onions (300g), cut into wedges

⅓ cup (80ml) olive oil

1 tablespoon cracked black pepper

1 Combine cheese and egg in medium bowl; pour into greased 24cm springform tin. Drizzle cheese mixture with oil; sprinkle with chilli. Cover lightly with foil; bake in moderate oven about 50 minutes or until firm to touch. Remove foil, cook further 10 minutes or until browned.

2 Drain excess liquid from baked cheese. Cut cheese into wedges; serve with char-grilled vegetables.

char-grilled vegetables Combine ingredients in large bowl. Cook vegetables on heated oiled grill plate (or grill or barbecue) until browned and tender.

serves 8

per serving 27.6g fat; 1500kJ

barbecued, char-grilled and roasted vegetables

Mixed baked vegetables with rosemary and garlic, char-grilled salad with polenta rounds and pesto, and lemon roasted onions and carrots are just a few of the mouth-watering meals you'll keep coming back to.

mixed baked vegetables
with rosemary and garlic

PREPARATION TIME 25 MINUTES ■ COOKING TIME 45 MINUTES

500g jap pumpkin, cut into
   1cm slices

500g desiree potatoes, cut into
   1cm slices

2 large zucchini (300g), cut into
   1cm strips

1 large yellow capsicum (350g),
   cut into 2cm strips

2 large leeks (450g), cut into
   1cm slices

2 tablespoons fresh rosemary

2 teaspoons cumin seeds

2 cloves garlic, crushed

2 tablespoons olive oil

1 tablespoon red-wine vinegar

60g fetta cheese

90g low-fat ricotta cheese

1 Combine pumpkin, potato, zucchini, capsicum and leek on large baking paper-lined baking tray. Add rosemary, seeds, garlic and oil; toss until combined.

2 Bake, uncovered, in moderately hot oven, about 45 minutes or until vegetables are browned lightly and tender, turning occasionally. Drizzle with vinegar.

3 Meanwhile, crumble fetta into small bowl. Add ricotta; stir until smooth.

4 Serve vegetables with cheese mixture.

serves 4

per serving 15g fat; 1409kJ

tip Soft fresh goat cheese can be substituted for fetta, if desired.

tossed vegetable salad
with lemon, garlic and pine nuts

PREPARATION TIME 20 MINUTES ■ COOKING TIME 10 MINUTES

vegan

250g asparagus

250g baby beans

2 small red capsicums (300g)

**4 baby eggplants (240g),
    halved lengthways**

2 tablespoons extra virgin olive oil

2 tablespoons lemon juice

**1/3 cup finely chopped fresh
    flat-leaf parsley**

1 clove garlic, crushed

1/2 teaspoon sambal oelek

1/4 cup (40g) toasted pine nuts

1 Halve asparagus spears; cut any thick pieces in half, lengthways.

2 Blanch asparagus and beans in boiling water about 1 minute or until just tender. Drain; rinse under cold water.

3 Cut capsicums into quarters; remove and discard seeds and membranes. Grill capsicum and eggplant on high about 3 minutes, each side, or until browned lightly and tender; cool to room temperature. Peel away skin from capsicum; slice capsicum thickly.

4 Place vegetables in large bowl. Add combined oil, juice, parsley, garlic and sambal oelek; toss to combine.

5 Serve sprinkled with pine nuts. Serve warm or at room temperature.

serves 6

per serving 9g fat; 492kJ
store Recipe can be made 3 hours ahead and refrigerated, covered.
tip Bake pine nuts on oven tray in moderate oven about 5 minutes or until toasted.

char-grilled salad
with polenta rounds and pesto

PREPARATION TIME 30 MINUTES (plus marinating time) ■ COOKING TIME 1 HOUR (plus standing time)

4 baby eggplants (240g)

4 small zucchini (360g)

2 baby fennel bulbs (250g), halved lengthways

250g cherry tomatoes

250g teardrop tomatoes

1/2 cup (125ml) lemon juice

1/2 cup (125ml) olive oil

4 cloves garlic, crushed

115g baby corn

400g baby carrots, trimmed

350g baby new potatoes, halved

polenta rounds

1/2 cup (125ml) vegetable stock

2 cups (500ml) water

1 cup (250ml) milk

1 1/2 cups (255g) polenta

20g butter

3/4 cup (60g) finely grated parmesan cheese

50g seeded black olives, chopped finely

pesto

1 3/4 cups firmly packed fresh basil

1 clove garlic, quartered

1/4 cup (40g) pine nuts, toasted

1/2 cup (40g) coarsely grated parmesan cheese

3/4 cup (180ml) olive oil

1 Slice eggplants and zucchini into three pieces, lengthways.

2 Combine eggplant, zucchini, fennel and tomatoes in large bowl with juice, oil and garlic. Cover; refrigerate 3 hours or overnight.

3 Place corn, carrot and potato in large oiled baking dish; bake, covered, in moderately hot oven 30 minutes, turning halfway during cooking.

4 Cook corn, carrot, potato and drained marinated vegetables, in batches, on heated oiled grill plate (or grill or barbecue) until browned and just tender.

5 Serve vegetables with polenta rounds and pesto.

polenta rounds Heat stock, the water and milk in large saucepan (do not boil). Add polenta; cook, stirring, about 2 minutes or until liquid is absorbed and mixture thickens. Stir in butter, cheese and olives. Spoon polenta into oiled 23cm-square slab cake pan; press firmly to ensure even thickness. When cool, cover; refrigerate about 3 hours or until firm. *[Can be made 1 day ahead to this stage and refrigerated, covered.]* Turn polenta onto board; cut into 12 rounds using a 5cm round cutter. Cook polenta on heated oiled grill plate (or grill or barbecue) until browned all over.

pesto Blend or process basil, garlic, pine nuts and cheese until almost smooth; with motor operating, gradually add oil until pesto is thickened and smooth.

serves 4

per serving 92.9g fat; 4600kJ

roasted root vegetables
with barley

PREPARATION TIME 20 MINUTES ■ COOKING TIME 1 HOUR 15 MINUTES

1 tablespoon olive oil

1 large brown onion (200g),
    sliced thinly

2 cloves garlic, crushed

3 medium carrots (360g),
    sliced into large pieces

3 medium parsnips (375g),
    sliced into large pieces

4 medium turnips (500g),
    sliced into large pieces

1/3 cup (80ml) honey

2 tablespoons dijon mustard

1/3 cup (80ml) lemon juice

1.5 litres (6 cups) vegetable stock

1 1/2 cups (300g) barley

1 tablespoon finely chopped
    fresh parsley

1 Heat oil in large flameproof baking dish; cook onion and garlic, stirring, until onion is soft. Add carrot, parsnip and turnip; cook, stirring, 1 minute.

2 Pour combined honey, mustard and juice over vegetables; bake, uncovered, in moderately hot oven about 1 1/4 hours or until vegetables are browned and tender.

3 Meanwhile, bring stock to a boil in large saucepan; add barley. Reduce heat; simmer, covered, about 25 minutes or until barley is tender and liquid is absorbed.

4 Just before serving, stir in parsley; serve topped with vegetables.

serves 4

per serving 8.4g fat; 2125kJ

roasted autumn vegetables
with toasted hazelnut dressing

PREPARATION TIME 20 MINUTES ■ COOKING TIME 30 MINUTES

500g baby beetroot

1 small swede (200g), quartered

2 small turnips (200g), quartered

1 small celeriac (1.25kg), quartered

2 medium carrots (240g),
halved lengthways

2 medium potatoes
(400g), quartered

2 medium parsnips (250g),
halved lengthways

2 teaspoons extra virgin olive oil

¼ cup (60ml) lemon juice

20g rocket leaves

20g lamb's lettuce

toasted hazelnut dressing

¼ cup (60ml) low-fat mayonnaise

2 tablespoons hazelnuts, toasted,
skins removed, crushed

2 teaspoons dijon mustard

2 teaspoons sherry vinegar

2 tablespoons vegetable stock

1 Combine beetroot, swede, turnip, celeriac, carrot, potato and parsnip in large baking dish; drizzle with oil and juice. Bake, uncovered, in hot oven about 30 minutes or until browned and tender.

2 Serve vegetables topped with rocket and lettuce; drizzle with toasted hazelnut dressing.

toasted hazelnut dressing Combine ingredients in small bowl; whisk well.

[Can be made 1 day ahead and refrigerated, covered.]

serves 6

per serving 5.9g fat; 943kJ
tip Baby spinach can be substituted for lamb's lettuce, if desired.

lemon roasted
onions and carrots

PREPARATION TIME 20 MINUTES ■ COOKING TIME 1 HOUR 10 MINUTES

vegan   **2 large brown onions (400g)**

2 medium lemons (280g)

5 small carrots (350g), halved

4 unpeeled cloves garlic

6 sprigs fresh rosemary

2 tablespoons olive oil

1 Cut onions and lemons into eight wedges.

2 Combine onion, lemon, carrot, garlic and rosemary in baking dish. Drizzle with oil; stir gently. Bake, uncovered, in moderate oven about 1 hour or until tender.

3 Increase oven temperature to hot; bake vegetables about 10 minutes or until browned.

serves 4

per serving 9.5g fat; 631kJ

Vegetable roast
herb & garlic dressing.

2 cloves garlic, crushed
1½ tbsp sweet chili sauce
⅓ cup tomato juice
1 tsp grated lemon rind
2 tbsp lemon juice
1 tsp tarragon dijon mustard
1½ tbsp olive oil

vegetable roast
with herb and garlic dressing

PREPARATION TIME 30 MINUTES ■ COOKING TIME 30 MINUTES

vegan

2 large red capsicums (700g)

2 large green capsicums (700g)

4 baby eggplants (240g), sliced thickly, lengthways

4 medium zucchini (480g), sliced thickly, lengthways

400g spring onions, halved

300g swiss brown mushrooms, halved

cooking-oil spray

herb and garlic dressing

¼ cup finely chopped fresh parsley

2 tablespoons finely chopped fresh mint

2 cloves garlic, crushed

1 fresh red chilli, seeded, chopped finely

⅓ cup (80ml) tomato juice

1 teaspoon grated lemon rind

2 tablespoons lemon juice

1½ tablespoons olive oil

1 teaspoon dijon mustard

1 Quarter capsicums; remove seeds and membranes. Place on oven trays, skin-side up, with eggplant, zucchini, spring onion and mushrooms; spray with a little cooking-oil spray. Bake, uncovered, in very hot oven about 20 minutes or until browned.

2 Turn eggplant, zucchini, onion and mushrooms; bake, uncovered, further 10 minutes or until browned and soft. Peel away skin from capsicum.

3 Serve vegetables with herb and garlic dressing.

herb and garlic dressing Combine ingredients in medium bowl; mix well.

[Can be made 3 hours ahead to this stage and refrigerated, covered.]

serves 4

per serving 9g fat; 884kJ

baked kumara,
shallots and squash with bean dip

PREPARATION TIME 20 MINUTES ■ COOKING TIME 45 MINUTES

**3 small kumara (750g),
cut into 1cm slices**

**250g golden shallots, peeled,
broken into segments**

**1 medium red capsicum
(200g), quartered**

500g yellow baby squash, halved

**6 medium egg tomatoes
(450g), halved**

2 teaspoons olive oil

6 sprigs thyme

3 cloves garlic, crushed

bean dip

**300g can butter beans,
rinsed, drained**

¼ cup (60g) tahini

**¼ cup (60ml)
low-fat yogurt**

**2 tablespoons coarsely
chopped chives**

2 teaspoons lemon juice

1 Place vegetables on baking paper-lined baking tray; brush with combined oil, thyme and garlic. Bake, uncovered, in moderately hot oven about 45 minutes or until tender. Turn vegetables, except tomato, occasionally.

2 Serve with bean dip and lemon wedges, if desired.

bean dip Mash beans in medium bowl; stir in tahini, yogurt, chives and juice. *[Can be made 1 day ahead and refrigerated, covered.]*

serves 4

per serving 12.8g fat; 1394kJ

herb and pine nut pie with
tomato coulis

PREPARATION TIME 40 MINUTES (plus refrigeration time) ■ COOKING TIME 1 HOUR 10 MINUTES

300g spinach, trimmed

1 small leek (200g), chopped finely

⅓ cup (50g) pine nuts

2 tablespoons finely chopped
    fresh chives

1 tablespoon finely chopped
    fresh thyme

1 tablespoon finely chopped
    fresh basil

3 eggs, beaten lightly

100g gruyere cheese,
    chopped finely

2 tablespoons grated fresh
    parmesan cheese

½ teaspoon cracked
    black peppercorns

⅓ cup (35g) packaged breadcrumbs

2 tablespoons white sesame seeds

1 egg, beaten lightly, extra

pastry

2¼ cups (335g) plain flour

180g butter

2 eggs, beaten lightly

tomato coulis

1 tablespoon olive oil

4 large tomatoes (1kg),
    chopped finely

½ cup (125ml) tomato puree

1 medium brown onion
    (150g), grated

1 sprig fresh thyme

1 bay leaf

1 teaspoon sugar

1 Steam or microwave spinach until wilted; drain. Squeeze spinach to remove excess liquid; chop finely.

2 Combine spinach, leek, pine nuts, herbs, egg, cheeses, peppercorns and breadcrumbs in large bowl; mix well.

3 Lightly grease oven tray; sprinkle with half of the sesame seeds. Cut pastry in half; roll out half of the pastry, between sheets of baking paper, into a 23cm circle. Place pastry on seeds on oven tray. Spoon filling onto centre of pastry leaving 2cm border; brush border lightly with water.

4 Roll out remaining pastry between sheets of baking paper into 25cm circle. Place over filling; pinch pastry edges together to seal. Brush pie with extra egg; sprinkle with remaining seeds. *[Can be made 3 hours ahead to this stage and refrigerated, covered.]*

5 Just before serving, bake pie, uncovered, in moderately hot oven about 40 minutes or until well browned and cooked through. Stand pie 5 minutes before serving.

6 Serve hot with tomato coulis.

pastry Place flour in medium bowl; rub in butter. Add egg; mix to a soft dough. Press dough into ball; knead gently on lightly floured surface until smooth. Cover; refrigerate about 30 minutes or until firm.

tomato coulis Heat oil in medium saucepan; cook remaining ingredients, uncovered, 40 minutes. Push mixture through sieve; discard pulp. Return liquid to pan; bring to a boil. Reduce heat; simmer, uncovered, about 20 minutes or until coulis thickens slightly. *[Can be made 2 days ahead to this stage and refrigerated, covered.]*

serves 8

per serving 36.3g fat; 2322kJ
store Uncooked pie and coulis can be frozen up to 6 months.

pies, pastries and pizzas

Tarts and flans have never been so easy.
Zucchini lentil pasties, and mushroom and leek tarts
are just a couple of the many delights to choose from.

spiced pumpkin
and coriander flans

PREPARATION TIME 40 MINUTES (plus refrigeration time) ■ COOKING TIME 40 MINUTES

1 cup (150g) plain flour

2 teaspoons ground coriander

90g butter

1 egg, beaten lightly

pumpkin filling

1 tablespoon peanut oil

1 medium brown onion (150g),
   chopped finely

1 clove garlic, crushed

1 tablespoon finely chopped
   fresh coriander

3 eggs, beaten lightly

½ cup (125ml) cream

½ cup (60g) grated swiss cheese

1 cup (400g) mashed pumpkin

1 Sift flour and coriander into medium bowl; rub in butter. Add enough of the egg to mix to a firm dough; knead on lightly floured surface until smooth. Cover; refrigerate about 30 minutes or until firm. Meanwhile, make pumpkin filling.

2 Roll pastry large enough to line six 10cm-deep flan tins; lift pastry into tins. Press into sides; trim edges. Place tins on oven tray; cover pastry with baking paper. Fill with dried beans or rice; bake, uncovered, in moderately hot oven 10 minutes. Remove paper and beans; bake, uncovered, further 7 minutes or until golden brown. Cool pastry cases. *[Can be made 1 day ahead to this stage and stored in airtight container.]*

3 Spoon pumpkin filling into pastry cases; bake, uncovered, in moderately hot oven about 15 minutes or until filling is set.

pumpkin filling Heat oil in medium frying pan. Cook onion, garlic and coriander, stirring, over medium heat about 2 minutes or until onion is soft; cool. Combine remaining ingredients in medium bowl; stir in cooled onion mixture.

makes 6

per serving 30.2g fat; 1761kJ

store Flans can be made 1 day ahead and refrigerated, covered.

tip You need to cook 500g pumpkin for this recipe.

onion tart

PREPARATION TIME 35 MINUTES (plus standing time) ■ COOKING TIME 1 HOUR 20 MINUTES (plus cooling time)

**5 large brown onions (1kg),
  sliced thinly**

2 tablespoons olive oil

60g butter

3 teaspoons thyme leaves

4 cloves garlic, crushed

**¼ cup (40g) finely chopped seeded
  black olives**

1½ cups (225g) plain flour

60g butter, chilled, extra

**2 tablespoons grated
  parmesan cheese**

125g cream cheese

1 egg

**2 tablespoons lemon
  juice, approximately**

150g goat cheese

1 Place onion in medium heatproof bowl; pour in enough boiling water to cover. Stand 15 minutes; drain well. Heat oil and butter in large heavy-base saucepan. Add onion; cook over low heat, stirring occasionally, about 20 minutes or until onion is very soft and golden brown.

2 Stir in thyme, garlic and olives; cook further 10 minutes on low. Let cool to room temperature.

3 Lightly grease 23cm flan tin. Process flour, extra butter, parmesan and half of the cream cheese until combined. Add egg and enough of the juice to make ingredients cling together.

4 Roll pastry large enough to line prepared tin; lift pastry into tin. Press into side; trim edge. Place tin on oven tray; cover pastry with baking paper. Fill with dried beans or rice; bake, uncovered, in moderately hot oven 10 minutes. Remove paper and beans; bake, uncovered, further 10 minutes or until golden brown. Cool pastry case.

5 Mix together remaining cream cheese and goat cheese; spread over base of pastry case. Top with onion mixture; bake, uncovered, in moderate oven about 30 minutes or until filling is firm. Serve at room temperature.

serves 6

per serving 36.7g fat; 2239kJ
store Tart can be made 2 days ahead and refrigerated, covered.
tip Frozen ready-rolled pastry sheets, joined with a little egg yolk, may be substituted for the pastry in this recipe, if preferred.

potato and herb pie

PREPARATION TIME 40 MINUTES (plus refrigeration time) ■ COOKING TIME 1 HOUR 30 MINUTES (plus cooling and standing time)

3 medium potatoes (600g), peeled

50g butter

¼ cup (60ml) olive oil

1 medium brown onion (150g), sliced thinly

2 tablespoons finely chopped fresh parsley

2 teaspoons finely chopped fresh thyme

½ cup (125ml) milk

½ cup (125ml) cream

2 eggs, beaten lightly, separately

1 sheet ready-rolled puff pastry

pastry

1 cup (150g) plain flour

90g butter, chilled

1 egg yolk

1 tablespoon lemon juice, approximately

1 Cut potatoes into 5mm slices.

2 Heat butter and oil in large saucepan; cook potato, in batches, until browned lightly and tender. Drain on absorbent paper; cool.

3 Cook onion in pan, stirring, until soft. Drain on absorbent paper; cool.

4 Layer potato, onion and herbs in pastry case; top with combined milk, cream and one egg. Brush edge of pastry case with a little of the remaining egg; top pie with puff pastry. Trim edges; press edges gently to seal. Brush pastry with remaining egg; prick pastry with fork.

5 Bake, uncovered, in moderately hot oven 15 minutes. Reduce heat to moderate; bake further 40 minutes or until pastry is puffed and browned. Stand pie 10 minutes before serving.

pastry Sift flour into large bowl; rub in butter. Add egg yolk and enough of the juice to mix to a firm dough. Press ingredients together to form a ball. Cover; refrigerate 30 minutes. Roll pastry between baking paper until large enough to line base and side of a 20cm springform tin. Ease pastry into tin; trim edge. Cover; refrigerate 20 minutes. Line pastry case with baking paper; fill with dried beans or rice. Bake, uncovered, in moderately hot oven 10 minutes; remove paper and beans. Bake, uncovered, further 10 minutes or until browned; cool.

serves 6

per serving 42.8g fat; 2381kJ
store Pie can be made 1 day ahead and refrigerated, covered.

mushroom,
eggplant and zucchini pizza

PREPARATION TIME 10 MINUTES ■ COOKING TIME 25 MINUTES

**200g button mushrooms,
    sliced thinly**

**2 medium zucchini (240g),
    sliced lengthways**

**1 baby eggplant (60g),
    sliced lengthways**

2 large pittas

½ x 140g tub pizza sauce

**½ cup (60g) finely grated
    cheddar cheese**

**2 teaspoons finely chopped
    fresh thyme**

1 Cook mushrooms, zucchini and eggplant, in batches, on heated oiled grill plate (or grill or barbecue) until browned lightly and just tender.

2 Place pittas on oven trays; spread evenly with pizza sauce. Sprinkle a quarter of the cheese over each pitta; top with mushroom, zucchini and eggplant. Sprinkle with remaining cheese; sprinkle with thyme.

3 Bake, uncovered, in very hot oven about 10 minutes or until pizzas are browned and crisp.

serves 4

per serving 6.4g fat; 818kJ

leek,
zucchini and carrot pies

PREPARATION TIME 20 MINUTES (plus refrigeration time) ■ COOKING TIME 35 MINUTES (plus cooling time)

1 cup (160g) wholemeal plain flour

70g butter, chilled, chopped coarsely

¼ cup (60ml) cold water, approximately

1 small leek (200g), sliced thinly

2 tablespoons plain flour

1 cup (250ml) skim milk

1 medium zucchini (120g), chopped finely

1 medium carrot (120g), chopped finely

1 tablespoon finely chopped fresh parsley

½ teaspoon skim milk, extra

1 Place wholemeal flour and 50g butter in food processor; process until combined. With motor operating, add enough of the water until mixture just forms a ball; knead lightly on floured surface until smooth. Cover; refrigerate 20 minutes.

2 Heat remaining butter in large saucepan. Stir in leek; cook until soft. Stir in flour; cook until bubbling. Remove from heat; gradually stir in milk. Stir over heat until sauce boils and thickens. Cover; cool to room temperature.

3 Boil, steam or microwave zucchini and carrot until just tender. Stir vegetables and parsley into sauce; spoon into two 1-cup (250ml) ovenproof dishes.

4 Roll pastry out on floured surface until 5mm thick. Cut pastry into two rounds large enough to cover dishes; trim edges. Brush with extra milk; decorate with remaining pastry. [Can be made 1 day ahead to this stage and refrigerated, covered.]

5 Bake, uncovered, in moderately hot oven about 20 minutes or until pastry is browned lightly and crisp.

serves 2

per serving 31.1g fat; 3901kJ

mushroom
and leek tarts

PREPARATION TIME 30 MINUTES (plus refrigeration time) ■ COOKING TIME 55 MINUTES

3/4 cup (110g) plain flour

55g butter, chilled

1 tablespoon seeded mustard

2 egg whites

1 tablespoon iced water, approximately

12 small button mushrooms (120g)

100g shiitake mushrooms

12 small swiss brown mushrooms (120g)

1 small leek (200g), sliced thinly

2 tablespoons fresh rosemary

2 egg whites, extra

2 eggs, beaten lightly

1/4 cup (60ml) skim milk

1 Place flour in small bowl; rub in butter until mixture resembles coarse breadcrumbs. Add mustard, egg whites and enough of the water to make ingredients cling together; knead on lightly floured surface until smooth. Cover; refrigerate about 30 minutes or until firm.

2 Roll pastry between sheets of baking paper until large enough to line six 12cm loose-bottom flan tins. Lift pastry into tins; press into sides. Trim edges; place tins on oven tray. Cover pastry with baking paper; fill with dried beans or rice. Bake, uncovered, in moderately hot oven, 10 minutes. Remove paper and beans; bake, uncovered, further 10 minutes or until browned lightly. Cool pastry cases. *[Can be made 1 day ahead to this stage and stored in airtight container.]*

3 Cook mushrooms in heated, lightly oiled large saucepan until browned lightly and softened. Stir in leek and rosemary; cook, stirring, until leek is soft. Divide mushroom mixture between pastry cases; pour over combined extra egg whites, egg and milk.

4 Bake, uncovered, in hot oven about 25 minutes or until firm.

serves 6

per serving 7.8g fat; 732kJ

zucchini lentil pasties

PREPARATION TIME 20 MINUTES (plus refrigeration time) ■ COOKING TIME 40 MINUTES (plus cooling time)

1 cup (160g) plain wholemeal flour

50g butter, chilled, chopped coarsely

¼ cup (60ml) cold water, approximately

1 medium brown onion (150g), chopped finely

2 cloves garlic, crushed

1 teaspoon mild curry powder

½ teaspoon grated fresh ginger

¼ teaspoon sambal oelek

¼ cup (50g) red lentils

⅔ cup (160ml) water, extra

1 medium zucchini (120g), grated finely

1 egg white

chilli and coriander sauce

2 large tomatoes (500g), chopped coarsely

¼ cup (60ml) water

⅓ cup (80ml) lime juice

¼ cup (50g) brown sugar

1 teaspoon fish sauce

⅓ cup (80ml) sweet chilli sauce

2 tablespoons finely chopped fresh coriander

1 Blend or process flour and butter until combined; with motor operating, add enough of the water until mixture just forms a ball. Knead lightly on floured surface until smooth. Cover; refrigerate about 20 minutes or until firm.

2 Meanwhile, cook onion, garlic, curry powder, ginger and sambal oelek, uncovered, in large non-stick saucepan 1 minute. Stir in lentils and the extra water; bring to a boil. Reduce heat; simmer, uncovered, about 10 minutes or until all liquid is absorbed. Remove from heat; stir in zucchini.

3 Roll out pastry on floured surface until 5mm thick; cut out six rounds using 12cm cutter. Divide filling among rounds; brush edges with some of the egg white. Fold rounds to enclose filling; pinch edges together to seal. Brush with remaining egg white; place on baking paper-covered oven tray. *[Can be made 1 day ahead to this stage and refrigerated, covered.]*

4 Bake, uncovered, in moderately hot oven about 25 minutes or until well browned. Serve with chilli and coriander sauce.

chilli and coriander sauce Combine tomato, the water, juice, sugar and sauces in medium saucepan; stir over low heat until sugar dissolves. Bring to a boil; reduce heat. Simmer, uncovered, about 10 minutes or until sauce thickens; remove from heat. Cool; stir in coriander.

makes 6

per serving 8.2g fat; 1017kJ
store Recipe can be frozen up to 6 months.

double potato pizza

PREPARATION TIME 25 MINUTES ■ COOKING TIME 25 MINUTES

1 medium brown onion (150g),
    sliced thinly

1 clove garlic, crushed

1 small kumara (250g), sliced thinly

2 medium potatoes (400g),
    sliced thinly

1 tablespoon tomato paste

1/4 cup (60ml) tomato puree

2 tablespoons fresh oregano

26cm pizza base (fresh or frozen)

2/3 cup (80g) grated
    reduced-fat cheddar

1 Place onion and garlic in small baking dish; bake, uncovered, in hot oven about 10 minutes or until browned lightly. Boil, steam or microwave kumara and potato separately until tender; drain.

2 Combine paste, puree and half of the oregano in small bowl; spread over pizza base.

3 Top pizza base with cheese, onion mixture, kumara, potato and remaining oregano.

4 Bake, uncovered, in hot oven about 15 minutes or until cheese melts.

serves 6

per serving 4.3g fat; 923kJ

vegetable pesto
pastries

PREPARATION TIME 15 MINUTES ■ COOKING TIME 20 MINUTES

2 sheets ready-rolled puff pastry, thawed
½ cup (125ml) sun-dried tomato pesto
280g jar antipasto char-grilled vegetables
6 medium egg tomatoes (450g), sliced lengthways
150g fetta cheese, crumbled

1 Cut pastry sheets in half. Place pastry pieces on two lightly greased oven trays. Fold pastry edges in to make 1cm border. Spread pesto over centre of pastry.

2 Drain vegetables; pat dry with absorbent paper. Cut vegetables into strips.

3 Arrange tomato and vegetables over centre of each piece of pastry; sprinkle with crumbled cheese.

4 Bake, uncovered, in very hot oven, 10 minutes. Swap shelf position of trays; bake further 10 minutes or until pastry is puffed and browned.

5 Top with fresh basil leaves, if desired.

serves 4

per serving 36.9g fat; 2309kJ

mushroom silverbeet strudel

PREPARATION TIME 30 MINUTES ■ COOKING TIME 35 MINUTES (plus cooling time)

640g trimmed silverbeet leaves

2 tablespoons vegetable oil

**300g button mushrooms,
    sliced thinly**

6 green onions, chopped finely

1/2 cup (100g) cottage cheese

1/4 teaspoon ground nutmeg

1 egg, beaten lightly

6 sheets fillo pastry

45g butter, melted

2 teaspoons packaged breadcrumbs

1 Boil, steam or microwave silverbeet until just wilted; drain. Squeeze excess liquid from silverbeet; chop finely.

2 Heat oil in medium saucepan; cook mushrooms and onion, stirring, over medium heat until mushrooms are soft. Drain; cool to room temperature.

3 Combine silverbeet and mushroom mixture in medium bowl with cheese, nutmeg and egg; mix well.

4 Layer sheets of pastry, brushing with butter between each layer. Spoon mushroom mixture along long edge of pastry; roll up like a swiss roll to enclose mixture, folding sides in as you roll.

5 Place strudel on oiled oven tray. Brush lightly with remaining butter; sprinkle with breadcrumbs. Bake, uncovered, in moderately hot oven about 25 minutes or until browned lightly.

serves 6

per serving 16g fat; 955kJ
tip Recipe best made just before serving.

zucchini and fetta spiral

PREPARATION TIME 40 MINUTES ■ COOKING TIME 35 MINUTES

2 tablespoons olive oil

1 medium brown onion (150g), sliced thinly

1 teaspoon ground caraway

3 medium (360g) zucchini, grated coarsely

1 medium (120g) carrot, grated coarsely

1 medium (200g) red capsicum, chopped finely

250g fetta cheese, crumbled

2 eggs, beaten lightly

14 sheets fillo pastry

125g butter, melted

1 egg, beaten lightly, extra

1 tablespoon grated parmesan cheese

1/2 teaspoon white sesame seeds

tomato sauce

1 tablespoon olive oil

1 medium brown onion (150g), sliced thinly

2 cloves garlic, sliced thinly

2 bay leaves

2 x 425g cans tomatoes

1 tablespoon tomato paste

1 teaspoon sugar

1/2 cup (125ml) water

1 Grease 31cm pizza pan. Heat oil in large frying pan; cook onion and caraway, stirring, until onion is soft. Add zucchini, carrot and capsicum; cook, stirring, until vegetables are soft and almost all liquid evaporates. Remove from heat; stir in fetta. Cool; stir in eggs. *[Can be made 1 day ahead to this stage and refrigerated, covered.]*

2 Layer two pastry sheets together, brushing each with butter. Spread 1/2 cup (125ml) vegetable mixture loosely down one long edge of pastry; leave 3cm border at each end. Roll pastry lightly around mixture, tucking in ends. Brush roll with butter; repeat with remaining pastry, butter and vegetable mixture.

3 Coil pastry rolls on pizza pan, starting from centre and working out to edge of pan to form a spiral, brushing sides of roll with extra egg as you work. Sprinkle with combined parmesan and seeds; bake, uncovered, in moderately hot oven about 20 minutes or until browned. Serve with tomato sauce.

tomato sauce Heat oil in medium saucepan; cook onion, garlic and bay leaves, stirring, until onion is soft. Add undrained crushed tomatoes, paste, sugar and the water; simmer, uncovered, about 25 minutes or until reduced by half. Discard bay leaves. *[Can be made 1 day ahead to this stage and refrigerated, covered.]*

serves 6

per serving 40.4g fat; 2310kJ
store Sauce can be frozen up to 6 months.

artichoke, olive and caper pizza

PREPARATION TIME 25 MINUTES (plus standing time) ■ COOKING TIME 20 MINUTES

¼ cup (60ml) tomato paste
3 x 285g jars artichoke hearts in oil, drained
1½ cups (240g) green olives, seeded, halved
¼ cup (50g) drained capers
¾ cup (60g) shaved parmesan cheese

pizza dough
2 teaspoons instant yeast
½ teaspoon salt
2½ cups (375g) plain flour
1 cup (250ml) warm water
2 teaspoons olive oil

1 Shape pizza dough into six 16cm rounds; place on greased oven trays.

2 Divide paste among pizza bases; spread over evenly.

3 Grill artichokes until browned lightly on both sides. Place artichokes, olives and capers on pizza bases; sprinkle with cheese.

4 Bake, uncovered, in moderately hot oven about 20 minutes or until bases are crisp.

pizza dough Combine yeast, salt and flour in large bowl; mix well. Gradually stir in combined water and oil. Knead lightly on work surface about 10 minutes or until well combined and dough springs back when pressed. Place dough in oiled large bowl; cover. Stand in warm place about 30 minutes or until dough doubles in bulk. Knead dough on work surface until smooth; use as required.

serves 6

per serving 31.1g fat; 3901kJ

eggplant and mushroom
pastitsio

PREPARATION TIME 25 MINUTES ■ COOKING TIME 1 HOUR 15 MINUTES

¼ cup (60ml) olive oil

1 medium eggplant (300g), cut into
  2cm pieces

1 medium brown onion (150g),
  chopped finely

2 cloves garlic, crushed

200g button mushrooms, halved

2 x 410g cans tomatoes

½ cup (125ml) dry red wine

1½ cups (375ml) vegetable stock

250g penne

1½ cups (185g) grated tasty cheese

pinch ground nutmeg

cream sauce

2 cups (400g) ricotta cheese, sieved

3 eggs, beaten lightly

1 cup (250ml) cream

¾ cup (90g) grated tasty cheese

⅓ cup (25g) grated
  parmesan cheese

1 Heat 2 tablespoons of the oil in large saucepan. Cook eggplant until browned
   lightly; drain on absorbent paper.

2 Add remaining oil to pan; cook onion, garlic and mushrooms, stirring, until
   onion is soft.

3 Combine undrained crushed tomatoes, wine and stock in another large
   saucepan; simmer, uncovered, stirring occasionally, about 10 minutes or until
   thick. Stir in eggplant and mushroom mixture.

4 Cook pasta in large saucepan of boiling water, uncovered, until just
   tender; drain.

5 Combine pasta with half of the eggplant mixture. Spread into 2.5-litre (10-cup)
   ovenproof dish; top with remaining eggplant mixture. Spread with cream
   sauce; sprinkle with cheese and nutmeg.

6 Bake, uncovered, in moderate oven about 40 minutes or until heated through
   and browned.

cream sauce Combine ingredients in large bowl; mix well.

serves 4

per serving 83.6g fat; 5057kJ
store Pastitsio can be made 1 day ahead and refrigerated, covered.

pasta and noodles

Expand your cooking repertoire with creative new combinations including sichuan spaghetti and tagliatelle with mushrooms and peppercorn brie.

fettuccine with
roasted mushrooms and tomato

PREPARATION TIME 20 MINUTES ■ COOKING TIME 20 MINUTES

200g flat mushrooms

200g button mushrooms

200g swiss brown mushrooms

250g cherry tomatoes

½ cup (125ml) vegetable stock

2 teaspoons garlic salt

375g fettuccine

¼ cup torn fresh basil

¼ cup (20g) coarsely grated parmesan cheese

1 Cut flat mushrooms into quarters.

2 Combine mushrooms, tomatoes and stock in baking dish; sprinkle with salt.

3 Bake, uncovered, in hot oven, about 20 minutes or until mushrooms are tender and tomatoes softened.

4 Meanwhile, cook pasta in large saucepan of boiling water, uncovered, until just tender; drain.

5 Gently toss mushroom mixture through pasta; sprinkle with basil and cheese.

serves 4

per serving 3.7g fat; 1664kJ

baked penne
with peas, mushrooms and leek

PREPARATION TIME 15 MINUTES ■ COOKING TIME 1 HOUR 10 MINUTES

400g penne

2 tablespoons vegetable oil

50g butter

1 clove garlic, crushed

2 small leeks (400g), sliced thinly

**300g button mushrooms,
   sliced thinly**

1/3 cup finely chopped fresh chives

2 cups (250g) frozen peas, thawed

bechamel sauce

100g butter

2/3 cup (100g) plain flour

1.25 litres (5 cups) hot milk

**2 1/2 cups (310g) coarsely grated
   cheddar cheese**

1 Cook pasta in large saucepan of boiling water, uncovered, until just tender; drain.

2 Heat oil and butter in medium frying pan; cook garlic, leek and mushrooms, stirring, until leek softens.

3 Combine pasta and leek mixture in large bowl with chives and peas. Reserve 2/3 cup bechamel sauce for top. Stir remaining sauce into leek mixture.

4 Spoon leek mixture into 3.75 litre (15-cup) ovenproof dish; spread with reserved bechamel sauce. *[Can be made 1 day ahead to this stage and refrigerated, covered.]*

5 Bake, uncovered, in moderate oven about 40 minutes or until browned lightly.

bechamel sauce Melt butter in medium saucepan; cook flour, stirring, until mixture thickens and bubbles. Gradually stir in milk; stir until sauce boils and thickens. Remove from heat; stir in cheese.

serves 6

per serving 53.7g fat; 3816kJ

pistachio pesto with
eggplant lasagne

PREPARATION TIME 55 MINUTES (plus standing time) ■ COOKING TIME 1 HOUR 40 MINUTES

3 medium eggplants (900g), cut into 1cm slices

¼ cup (60ml) olive oil

4 medium red capsicums (800g)

750g jar pasta sauce

250g packet instant lasagne sheets

250g mozzarella cheese, sliced thinly

pistachio pesto

½ cup (75g) shelled pistachios

1 cup firmly packed fresh basil

⅓ cup (80ml) olive oil

2 cloves garlic, crushed

2 tablespoons grated parmesan cheese

white sauce

80g butter

⅓ cup (50g) plain flour

2½ cups (625ml) milk

½ cup (40g) grated parmesan cheese

1 Oil 6cm-deep rectangular 3.5 litre (14-cup) ovenproof dish.

2 Place eggplant in colander. Sprinkle with salt; stand 20 minutes. Rinse eggplant under cold running water; drain on absorbent paper.

3 Brush eggplant with oil; place in single layer on two oven trays. Bake, uncovered, in moderately hot oven about 40 minutes or until browned and tender.

4 Meanwhile, quarter capsicums; remove and discard seeds and membranes. Roast under grill or in very hot oven, skin-side up, until skin blisters and blackens; cover capsicum pieces in plastic or paper 5 minutes. Peel away skin; cut capsicum pieces into thick strips.

5 Spread a third of the pasta sauce into prepared dish. Top with a third of the lasagne, another third of the sauce, half of the eggplant, half of the cheese, another third of the lasagne, then remaining sauce, capsicum, cheese, lasagne and eggplant. Spread pistachio pesto over eggplant; top with white sauce.

6 Cover lasagne with foil; bake, in moderate oven 30 minutes. Remove foil; bake 30 minutes or until browned lightly. Stand 5 minutes before serving.

pistachio pesto Blend or process ingredients until pureed.

white sauce Heat butter in medium saucepan; cook flour, stirring, until mixture thickens and bubbles. Gradually stir in milk; stir until mixture boils and thickens. Remove from heat; stir in cheese.

serves 6

per serving 52g fat; 3508kJ
store Lasagne can be made 1 day ahead and refrigerated, covered.

sichuan spaghetti

PREPARATION TIME 10 MINUTES ▪ COOKING TIME 25 MINUTES

vegan

450g spaghetti

4 spring onions, chopped finely

3 cloves garlic, crushed

1/3 cup (80ml) vegetable stock

1 teaspoon cornflour

1/3 cup (80ml) soy sauce

1 tablespoon rice wine vinegar

1 tablespoon sichuan hot bean paste

1 teaspoon raw sugar

1/3 cup (75g) vegetarian bacon, chopped finely

1/4 cup (35g) finely chopped roasted peanuts

250g spinach, trimmed, chopped finely

1/2 lebanese cucumber (65g), peeled, chopped finely

1 Place pasta in large saucepan of boiling water. Boil, uncovered, until just tender; drain.

2 Meanwhile heat lightly oiled wok or large frying pan; stir-fry onion and garlic until onion is soft. Add blended stock, cornflour, sauce, vinegar, paste and sugar; stir until mixture boils and thickens.

3 Stir in bacon, peanuts and spinach; cook until spinach wilts and mixture is hot.

4 Serve pasta with spinach mixture and cucumber.

serves 6

per serving 6.5g fat; 1501kJ

tip Chinese chilli paste can be substituted for sichuan hot bean paste, if unavailable.

marinated tofu
and bok choy stir-fry

PREPARATION TIME 15 MINUTES ■ COOKING TIME 15 MINUTES (plus marinating time)

350g firm tofu, drained, cut into 2cm cubes

2 teaspoons peanut oil

1 large white onion (200g), sliced thinly

1 medium red capsicum (200g), sliced thinly

200g snow peas, trimmed

¼ cup (60ml) vegetable stock

400g bok choy, shredded

420g thin fresh egg noodles

marinade

¼ cup (60ml) hoisin sauce

¼ cup (60ml) oyster sauce

1 tablespoon soy sauce

1 teaspoon grated fresh ginger

2 cloves garlic, crushed

1 Combine tofu and marinade in large bowl. Cover; refrigerate 3 hours or overnight. *[Can be made 1 day ahead to this stage and refrigerated, covered.]*

2 Heat oil in wok or large frying pan; stir-fry onion and capsicum until tender. Add peas and stock; cook, stirring, until hot.

3 Add bok choy, noodles and undrained tofu to wok; stir until hot.

marinade Combine ingredients in small bowl; mix well.

serves 4

per serving 11g fat; 2147kJ

sesame
noodle salad

PREPARATION TIME 25 MINUTES (plus standing time) ■ COOKING TIME 15 MINUTES

10 dried shiitake mushrooms (20g)

500g fresh thick egg noodles

6 baby eggplants (360g)

vegetable oil, for deep-frying

150g snow peas, halved

270g chinese broccoli

2 cups (100g) watercress sprigs

80g snow pea tendrils

70g oyster mushrooms

½ medium red capsicum (100g), sliced thinly

½ medium yellow capsicum (100g), sliced thinly

2 green onions, sliced thinly

¼ cup (35g) white sesame seeds, toasted

¼ cup firmly packed fresh coriander leaves

dressing

¼ cup (60ml) sweet chilli sauce

⅓ cup (80ml) soy sauce

¼ cup (60ml) balsamic vinegar

1½ tablespoons sugar

1½ tablespoons sesame oil

⅓ cup (80ml) vegetable oil

1 Place dried mushrooms in medium heatproof bowl; cover with boiling water. Stand 20 minutes; drain. Discard stems; slice mushrooms.

2 Add noodles to large saucepan of boiling water. Boil, uncovered, until just tender; drain. Rinse under cold water; drain.

3 Cut eggplants lengthways into 5mm slices. Deep-fry in hot oil until browned lightly; drain on absorbent paper.

4 Boil, steam or microwave snow peas and broccoli separately until just tender; drain. Rinse under cold water; drain.

5 Toss watercress in a little of the dressing; place on large plate.

6 Combine dried mushrooms, noodles, eggplant, snow peas, broccoli, tendrils, oyster mushrooms, capsicums, onion, seeds and coriander in large bowl. Pour over remaining dressing; mix well. Top watercress with noodle salad.

dressing Combine ingredients in screw-top jar; shake well. *[Can be made 3 days ahead and refrigerated, covered.]*

serves 6

per serving 25.6g fat; 2097kJ

eggplant, tomato and
leek lasagne

PREPARATION TIME 30 MINUTES ■ COOKING TIME 1 HOUR 20 MINUTES (plus standing time)

3 medium eggplants (900g)

coarse cooking salt

1 large brown onion (200g), chopped finely

4 cloves garlic, crushed

3 large tomatoes (750g), chopped coarsely

2 tablespoons tomato paste

¼ cup shredded fresh basil

20g butter

2 medium leeks (700g), chopped finely

2 tablespoons sugar

four 16cm x 30cm (200g) fresh lasagne sheets

1 cup (125g) grated low-fat cheddar cheese

1 Cut eggplants lengthways into 1cm slices; place slices in colander. Sprinkle with salt; stand 30 minutes. Rinse slices under cold running water; drain on absorbent paper.

2 Cook eggplant, in batches, in heated oiled large frying pan until softened and browned both sides.

3 Cook onion and half of the garlic in pan, stirring, until onion softens. Stir in tomato, paste and basil; simmer, uncovered, about 20 minutes or until thickened slightly. Blend or process tomato mixture until just combined.

4 Heat butter in pan; cook leek and remaining garlic, stirring, until leek is soft. Add sugar; cook, stirring about 5 minutes or until leek is browned lightly.

5 Cut one lasagne sheet to cover base of oiled deep 2.5 litre (10-cup) ovenproof dish. Top with a quarter of the eggplant, a quarter of the leek mixture, a quarter of the tomato mixture and a quarter of the cheese. Repeat layers three times, ending with cheese. *[Can be made 1 day ahead to this stage and refrigerated, covered.]*

6 Bake, uncovered, in moderately hot oven about 50 minutes or until heated through.

serves 6

per serving 11.1g fat; 1336kJ

pasta with tomatoes,
artichokes and olives

PREPARATION TIME 30 MINUTES ■ COOKING TIME 30 MINUTES

2 teaspoons olive oil

1 medium brown onion (150g), chopped finely

2 cloves garlic, crushed

¼ cup (60ml) dry white wine

2 x 425g cans tomatoes

2 tablespoons tomato paste

½ teaspoon sugar

½ cup (80g) seeded black olives

390g can artichoke hearts, drained, quartered

2 tablespoons finely sliced fresh basil leaves

375g spiral pasta

⅓ cup (25g) flaked parmesan cheese

1 Heat oil in large saucepan; cook onion and garlic, stirring, until onion softens. Add wine, undrained crushed tomatoes, paste and sugar; simmer, uncovered, about 15 minutes or until sauce thickens. Add olives, artichoke and basil; stir until hot.

2 Meanwhile, cook pasta in large saucepan of boiling water, uncovered, until just tender; drain.

3 Combine pasta with half of the sauce in large bowl; toss well. Serve pasta topped with remaining sauce and cheese.

serves 4

per serving 7g fat; 1928kJ

spicy tofu
with noodles

PREPARATION TIME 20 MINUTES ■ COOKING TIME 15 MINUTES

vegan

250g dried rice stick noodles

2 teaspoons chilli oil

6 green onions, sliced thinly

2 cloves garlic, crushed

250g asparagus, chopped coarsely

1 small red capsicum (150g), sliced thinly

2 tablespoons sweet chilli sauce

2 tablespoons light soy sauce

1 tablespoon black bean sauce

1 tablespoon rice wine vinegar

¼ cup (60ml) vegetable stock

190g packet fried tofu, chopped coarsely

500g spinach, trimmed, chopped coarsely

⅓ cup (50g) unsalted roasted peanuts

1 Place noodles in large heatproof bowl; cover with boiling water. Stand until just tender; drain. Rinse under cold water; drain.

2 Heat oil in wok or large frying pan; stir-fry onion, garlic, asparagus and capsicum until just tender. Add noodles, sauces, vinegar and stock; stir-fry until sauce boils.

3 Add tofu and spinach; stir-fry until spinach just wilts. Serve topped with nuts.

serves 4

per serving 12.4g fat; 1543kJ

tagliatelle with mushrooms and
peppercorn brie

PREPARATION TIME 15 MINUTES ■ COOKING TIME 25 MINUTES

400g tagliatelle

**200g peppercorn brie
cheese, chilled**

60g butter

6 green onions, chopped finely

2 cloves garlic, crushed

**300g button mushrooms,
sliced thinly**

200g flat mushrooms, sliced thinly

½ cup (125ml) dry white wine

1 cup (250ml) vegetable stock

1 tablespoon seeded mustard

**¼ cup (25g) drained sun-dried
tomatoes, sliced thinly**

1 cup (250ml) cream

**2 teaspoons finely chopped
fresh thyme**

1 Cook pasta in large saucepan of boiling water; boil, uncovered, until just tender.

2 Meanwhile, remove rind from cheese; slice cheese thinly.

3 Heat butter in large saucepan; cook onion, garlic and mushrooms, stirring, until mushrooms are soft.

4 Add wine and stock; simmer, uncovered, until liquid reduces by half.

5 Add mustard, tomato, cheese, cream and thyme; stir until cheese melts.

6 Drain pasta; serve with sauce.

serves 4

per serving 58.3g fat; 4081kJ

penne primavera

PREPARATION TIME 25 MINUTES ■ COOKING TIME 15 MINUTES

2 tablespoons olive oil

375g penne pasta

1 large onion (200g), chopped finely

2 cloves garlic, crushed

4 baby carrots (50g), chopped finely

150g green beans, chopped finely

100g snow peas, trimmed, halved

250g asparagus, chopped coarsely

1 tablespoon fresh oregano

2 teaspoons fresh thyme

400g can diced tomatoes

1¼ cups (100g) shaved parmesan cheese

1 Add half of the oil to large saucepan of boiling water. Cook pasta, uncovered, until just tender; drain.

2 Meanwhile, heat remaining oil in large frying pan. Cook onion, stirring occasionally, over low heat, until onion is very soft but not browned. Add garlic and carrot; cook, stirring, 1 minute. Stir in beans; cook until changed in colour. Stir in snow peas and asparagus; cook until changed in colour. Add herbs and tomato; bring to a boil. Reduce heat; simmer until heated through and thickened slightly.

3 Toss pasta through hot sauce; serve with cheese.

serves 4

per serving 18.7g fat; 2364kJ

tip Make dish ahead of time; top with mixture of parmesan cheese, mozzarella cheese, cheddar cheese and stale breadcrumbs. Bake in moderate oven about 30 minutes or until heated through.

wheat noodle, snake bean

and roasted capsicum salad

PREPARATION TIME 20 MINUTES ▪ COOKING TIME 20 MINUTES

vegan

3 medium red capsicums (600g)
250g dried wheat noodles
350g snake beans, cut into 4cm lengths
1 medium red onion (170g), sliced thinly
2 tablespoons white sesame seeds, toasted
1/2 cup coarsely chopped fresh coriander

sesame-soy dressing
1/4 cup (60ml) lemon juice
1/3 cup (80ml) peanut oil
1 teaspoon sesame oil
2 tablespoons rice wine vinegar
2 tablespoons soy sauce
1 tablespoon brown sugar

1 Quarter capsicums; remove and discard seeds and membranes. Grill capsicum, skin-side up, until skin blisters and blackens. Cover capsicum quarters in plastic or paper 5 minutes. Peel away skin; cut each quarter in half lengthways. Cut pieces into thick diagonal slices. *[Can be made 1 day ahead to this stage and refrigerated, covered.]*

2 Meanwhile, cook noodles in large saucepan of boiling water, uncovered, until just tender; drain.

3 Boil, steam or microwave beans until just tender; drain.

4 Gently toss capsicum, noodles, beans, onion, seeds and coriander in large bowl with sesame-soy dressing.

sesame-soy dressing Combine ingredients in screw-top jar; shake well.

serves 4

per serving 24g fat; 2117kJ

tofu and pumpkin soup

vegan

PREPARATION TIME 15 MINUTES
COOKING TIME 30 MINUTES

1 litre (4 cups) vegetable stock
500g pumpkin, peeled, chopped coarsely
2 teaspoons grated fresh ginger
200g silken tofu
1 tablespoon finely chopped
** fresh coriander**

1 Combine stock, pumpkin and ginger in large saucepan; bring to a boil. Reduce heat; simmer, uncovered, about 25 minutes or until pumpkin is very soft.

2 Blend pumpkin mixture, in batches, with tofu until smooth and combined. Return to pan; reheat gently. Stir in coriander just before serving.

serves 6

per serving 3.2g fat; 345kJ
store Soup can be made 2 days ahead and refrigerated in airtight container.

tempeh with thai bean curry

PREPARATION TIME 5.MINUTES
COOKING TIME 15 MINUTES

600g tempeh
1 tablespoon peanut oil
2 medium onions (300g), sliced thinly
2 cloves garlic, crushed
175g baby beans or green beans,
** trimmed, halved**
¼ cup (60ml) thai red curry paste
400ml can coconut milk

1 Cut tempeh into 5cm x 7cm slices. Heat oil in medium frying pan; cook tempeh until well browned all over. Remove from pan; keep warm.

2 Cook onion in pan, over low heat, about 10 minutes or until very soft. Add garlic and beans; cook, stirring occasionally, until beans just change in colour. Stir in curry paste and coconut milk; bring to a boil. Reduce heat; simmer, uncovered, about 5 minutes or until thickened slightly.

3 Serve bean curry over tempeh slices.

serves 4

per serving 38.3g fat; 2282kJ

tofu pesto

vegan PREPARATION TIME 10 MINUTES

1 cup firmly packed basil leaves
100g silken tofu, chopped finely
3 cloves garlic, crushed
¼ cup (40g) pine nuts, toasted
⅓ cup (80ml) olive oil

1 Blend or process ingredients until smooth.
Serve over hot pasta or add to salad
dressings, if desired.

makes 1 cup (250ml)

per tablespoon 12.4g fat; 491kJ
store Spoon pesto into hot sterilised jars. Pour a
thin layer of olive oil over pesto to stop mixture
becoming dark; seal. Pesto can be made 1 week
ahead and refrigerated.

herbed tofu dip

vegan PREPARATION TIME 10 MINUTES (plus standing time)

300g firm tofu
3 cloves garlic, chopped finely
3 teaspoons finely chopped fresh thyme
2 tablespoons peanut oil
1 tablespoon lemon juice

1 Blend ingredients about 5 minutes or until
smooth and well combined. Spoon mixture
into serving dish. Cover; refrigerate 1 hour.

makes 1 cup (250ml)

per tablespoon 4.8g fat; 236kJ
store Dip can be made 1 day ahead and
refrigerated, covered.

tofu
with chilli peanut sauce

PREPARATION TIME 10 MINUTES ■ COOKING TIME 40 MINUTES

vegan

vegetable oil, for deep-frying

500g packet firm tofu, drained, chopped coarsely

1 tablespoon peanut oil

2 small red capsicums (300g), sliced thinly

160g sugar snap peas

300g spinach, trimmed

2 cups (160g) bean sprouts

2 cloves garlic, crushed

3 red thai chillies, sliced thinly

2 teaspoons sambal oelek

1/4 cup (70g) crunchy peanut butter

2 teaspoons palm sugar

1 tablespoon chinese rice wine

1 tablespoon hoisin sauce

1 tablespoon thick sweet soy sauce

1 tablespoon mild sweet chilli sauce

3/4 cup (180ml) water

1/3 cup (50g) unsalted roasted peanuts

4 green onions, chopped finely

1 tablespoon finely chopped fresh coriander

1 Heat vegetable oil in wok or large frying pan. Deep-fry tofu, in batches, until browned; drain on absorbent paper.

2 Heat peanut oil in wok; stir-fry capsicum, peas, spinach and sprouts until just tender. Remove; cover to keep warm.

3 Add garlic and chilli to wok; stir-fry until fragrant. Add combined sambal oelek, peanut butter, sugar, wine, sauces, water and peanuts; stir over heat until sauce boils.

4 Add onion, coriander and tofu; stir until hot.

5 Serve tofu and sauce on vegetables.

serves 4

per serving 35.7g fat; 2138kJ

meals in minutes

Time need no longer be a factor when choosing a recipe. Each of these convenient meals can be made in under 40 minutes, including curried squash with mushrooms and spanish tortilla with spicy tomato sauce.

spiced chickpeas
with tomatoes

PREPARATION TIME 10 MINUTES ■ COOKING TIME 20 MINUTES

1 tablespoon ghee

2 medium brown onions (300g), chopped finely

2 cloves garlic, crushed

2 teaspoons ground cumin

2 teaspoons ground coriander

1/4 teaspoon cardamom seeds

1 teaspoon chilli powder

1 large kumara (500g), chopped coarsely

2 cups (500ml) vegetable stock

1 tablespoon tomato paste

300g can chickpeas, rinsed, drained

4 medium tomatoes (760g), peeled, seeded, chopped finely

1/3 cup (65g) red lentils, rinsed

2 tablespoons finely chopped fresh coriander

1 Heat ghee in large saucepan; cook onion and garlic, stirring, until onion softens. Add spices; stir over heat until fragrant.

2 Add kumara, stock, paste, chickpeas, tomato and lentils; simmer, covered, about 15 minutes or until lentils are soft. Stir in coriander.

3 Serve with low-fat yogurt, extra coriander and couscous, if desired.

serves 4

per serving 7.3g fat; 1095kJ

store Spiced chickpeas with tomatoes can be made 2 days ahead and refrigerated, covered.

ginger noodles

PREPARATION TIME 15 MINUTES ■ COOKING TIME 20 MINUTES

375g thick fresh egg noodles

2 medium carrots (240g)

2 medium zucchini (240g)

1 tablespoon peanut oil

**1 medium red capsicum (200g),
chopped coarsely**

1 clove garlic, crushed

1 tablespoon grated fresh ginger

500g bok choy, shredded coarsely

425g can baby corn, drained, halved

2 tablespoons green ginger wine

2 tablespoons hoisin sauce

1 tablespoon soy sauce

2 teaspoons cornflour

1 tablespoon water

1 Cook noodles in large saucepan of boiling water, uncovered, until just tender; drain.

2 Using vegetable peeler, peel long thin strips from carrots and zucchini.

3 Heat oil in wok or large frying pan; stir-fry carrot, zucchini, capsicum, garlic and ginger until carrot is just tender.

4 Add bok choy and corn; stir-fry until bok choy just wilts.

5 Add noodles, wine, sauces, and blended cornflour and water; stir until sauce boils and thickens slightly.

serves 4

per serving 7.3g fat; 1975kJ

double pea
and tofu with pistachios

PREPARATION TIME 10 MINUTES ■ COOKING TIME 20 MINUTES

2 tablespoons peanut oil
600g firm tofu, drained, roughly chopped
1 cup (150g) pistachios, shelled
30g butter
2 cloves garlic, crushed
2 red thai chillies, seeded, chopped finely
2 teaspoons grated fresh ginger
400g sugar snap peas, trimmed
400g snow peas, trimmed
¼ cup (60ml) sweet chilli sauce

1 Heat half of the oil in wok or large frying pan; stir-fry tofu and nuts, in batches, until tofu is browned lightly.

2 Heat remaining oil with butter in wok; stir-fry garlic, chilli and ginger until mixture is fragrant.

3 Add peas to wok; stir-fry until just tender.

4 Return tofu and nuts to wok with sauce; stir-fry, tossing to combine ingredients.

serves 4

per serving 45.5g fat; 2692kJ

curried squash
with mushrooms

PREPARATION TIME 15 MINUTES ■ COOKING TIME 10 MINUTES

vegan

1 tablespoon peanut oil

1 clove garlic, crushed

1 teaspoon ground cumin

1 teaspoon ground caraway

1 teaspoon ground nutmeg

1 teaspoon mild curry powder

1/2 teaspoon ground turmeric

1 medium brown onion (150g),
   sliced thinly

1 medium carrot (120g), sliced thinly

300g yellow squash, quartered

1 medium green capsicum (200g),
   sliced thinly

200g button mushrooms, halved

1 teaspoon cornflour

3/4 cup (180ml) coconut cream

1 tablespoon finely chopped
   fresh coriander

1 Heat oil in wok or large frying pan; stir-fry garlic and spices until fragrant.

2 Add onion and carrot; stir-fry until onion is soft. Add squash, capsicum and mushrooms; stir-fry.

3 Add blended cornflour and coconut cream; stir until mixture boils and thickens slightly. Serve sprinkled with coriander.

serves 4

per serving 14.5g fat; 824kJ

store Curry can be made 1 day ahead and refrigerated, covered.

bean and potato
bake

PREPARATION TIME 10 MINUTES ■ COOKING TIME 25 MINUTES

4 small potatoes (480g), peeled, sliced thinly

2 green onions, sliced thinly

½ x 420g can Mexe-beans

½ cup (125ml) skim milk

¼ cup (20g) grated parmesan cheese

1 Layer potato, onion and beans in two 1-cup (250ml) lightly greased ovenproof dishes. Pour milk over vegetables; sprinkle with cheese.

2 Bake, uncovered, in moderate oven about 25 minutes or until vegetables are soft.

serves 2

per serving 3.8g fat; 1008kJ

quartet of beans
in chilli lime sauce

PREPARATION TIME 10 MINUTES ■ COOKING TIME 20 MINUTES

vegan

270g rice stick noodles

250g frozen broad beans, thawed, peeled

150g green beans, halved

150g snake beans, chopped coarsely

150g butter beans, halved

vegetable oil, for deep-frying

¼ cup (40g) capers, drained

1 tablespoon olive oil

6 cloves garlic, crushed

1 small red onion (100g), cut into wedges

4 red thai chillies, seeded

2 tablespoons finely grated lime rind

1 cup (250ml) vegetable stock

1 Place noodles in medium heatproof bowl; cover with boiling water. Stand until just tender; drain. Rinse under cold water; drain.

2 Meanwhile, boil, steam or microwave beans, separately, until just tender; drain. Heat vegetable oil in small frying pan; deep-fry capers until crisp. Drain on absorbent paper.

3 Heat olive oil in wok or large frying pan; stir-fry garlic, onion, chilli and rind until onion is soft.

4 Add stock, beans and noodles; cook, stirring gently, until sauce thickens and mixture is hot.

5 Serve topped with capers.

serves 4

per serving 6.7g fat; 1326kJ

tip Bean thread noodles can be substituted for rice stick noodles.

chinese water spinach with
crispy noodles

PREPARATION TIME 10 MINUTES ▪ COOKING TIME 5 MINUTES

vegan

360g chinese water spinach

**2 trimmed sticks celery (150g),
    sliced thinly**

250g cherry tomatoes, halved

6 green onions, sliced thinly

100g packet fried noodles

**1/3 cup (35g) pecans, toasted,
    sliced thinly**

soy and chilli dressing

1/4 cup (60ml) peanut oil

2 tablespoons white vinegar

2 tablespoons sweet chilli sauce

1 tablespoon soy sauce

1/2 teaspoon sesame oil

1 Boil, steam or microwave spinach until just wilted; drain.

2 Combine spinach and remaining ingredients in large bowl. Add soy and chilli dressing; toss gently.

soy and chilli dressing Combine ingredients in screw-top jar; shake well.

[Can be made 3 days ahead and refrigerated, covered.]

serves 6

per serving 16.3g fat; 805kJ

spaghetti
with pesto sauce

PREPARATION TIME 10 MINUTES ▓ COOKING TIME 10 MINUTES

2 cups (160g) fresh basil

1 clove garlic, crushed

1/3 cup (25g) grated parmesan cheese

1 tablespoon olive oil

1 tablespoon no-oil light french dressing

250g spaghetti

1 Blend or process basil, garlic, cheese, oil and dressing until well combined.

2 Cook pasta in large saucepan of boiling water, uncovered, until just tender; drain.

3 Toss pesto through pasta before serving.

serves 2

per serving 15.6g fat; 2512kJ

store Pesto can be made 3 days ahead and refrigerated, covered.

pasta carbonara
with vegetables

PREPARATION TIME 15 MINUTES ■ COOKING TIME 20 MINUTES

¾ cup spiral or other pasta

1 tablespoon olive oil

1 small red onion (100g), sliced thickly

½ medium red capsicum (100g), chopped finely

80g snow peas, chopped finely

60g mushrooms, chopped finely

100g drained canned corn kernels

¼ cup (20g) grated parmesan cheese

¼ cup (30g) grated tasty cheese

½ cup (125ml) sour cream

2 eggs, beaten lightly

½ teaspoon garlic salt

1 tablespoon coarsely chopped fresh chives

1 tablespoon finely chopped fresh basil

1 Cook pasta, uncovered, in large saucepan of boiling water until just tender; drain.

2 Meanwhile heat oil in large saucepan; cook onion, capsicum, snow peas and mushrooms, stirring, until onion is soft.

3 Add pasta, corn, cheeses and sour cream; stir until combined and heated through.

4 Remove from heat; stir in eggs, salt and herbs. Stir until combined and thickened slightly.

serves 2

per serving 48.1g fat; 3138kJ

spanish tortilla
with spicy tomato sauce

PREPARATION TIME 10 MINUTES ■ COOKING TIME 25 MINUTES (plus standing time)

4 medium potatoes (800g)

¹⁄₃ cup (80ml) olive oil

5 eggs, beaten lightly

1 medium brown onion (150g), chopped finely

2 cloves garlic, crushed

400g can tomatoes

1 teaspoon mexican chilli powder

1 Boil, steam or microwave potatoes until just tender; drain. Slice potatoes thinly.

2 Heat 1 tablespoon of the oil in 24cm non-stick frying pan. Arrange potato in pan; pour eggs over potato. Cook, tilting pan, over medium heat until omelette is almost set; drizzle 1 tablespoon of the oil over omelette. Place pan under heated grill until top is browned; stand 5 minutes. Turn onto serving platter; keep warm.

3 Heat remaining oil in pan; cook onion and garlic, stirring, until onion is soft. Add undrained crushed tomatoes and chilli powder; cook, uncovered, about 5 minutes or until sauce thickens. Serve sauce with tortilla.

serves 4

per serving 25.3g fat; 1742kJ

southern-style cabbage
with sweet potato scones

PREPARATION TIME 15 MINUTES ■ COOKING TIME 25 MINUTES

2 cups (500ml) water

1 medium brown onion (150g),
   chopped finely

1 bay leaf

1/2 teaspoon allspice

1/4 teaspoon ground cumin

2 cloves garlic, crushed

1 tablespoon worcestershire sauce

2 teaspoons tamari

2 teaspoons honey

500g savoy cabbage, sliced thickly

500g purple cabbage, sliced thickly

1 tablespoon extra virgin olive oil

1/2 teaspoon cayenne pepper

sweet potato scones

400g white sweet potato,
   chopped coarsely

2/3 cup (160ml) soy milk

2 teaspoons lemon juice

1 cup (160g) plain wholemeal flour

1 cup (150g) plain flour

1 tablespoon baking powder

1 teaspoon bicarbonate of soda

1 tablespoon raw sugar

1/2 teaspoon salt

1/4 cup (60ml) safflower oil

1 Combine the water, onion, bay leaf, allspice, cumin, garlic, sauce, tamari and honey in medium saucepan; cover. Bring to a boil; reduce heat. Simmer, uncovered, 5 minutes.

2 Add cabbages; cook, uncovered, further 5 minutes or until tender, stirring occasionally.

3 Remove bay leaf; stir in oil and pepper.

serves 4

per serving 5.4g fat; 496kJ

sweet potato scones Preheat oven to 210°C. Boil or steam sweet potato in medium saucepan until tender; drain. Mash; cool. Combine soy milk and juice, stand 10 minutes or until milk thickens slightly (it will resemble buttermilk). Place wholemeal flour in large bowl; add plain flour, baking powder, soda, sugar and salt. Add sweet potato, soy milk and oil; combine to form a soft dough. Turn onto a lightly floured surface; knead until just smooth. Press out until dough is about 3cm thick; cut into 8cm squares. Place squares 1cm apart on baking paper covered baking tray. Bake 15 minutes or until golden brown, serve warm or cold.

makes 12

per scone 5.6g fat; 679kJ

curried eggs

PREPARATION TIME 10 MINUTES ■ COOKING TIME 20 MINUTES

¹/₄ cup (60ml) peanut oil
8 hard-boiled eggs
1 teaspoon black mustard seeds
1 clove garlic, crushed
1 teaspoon grated fresh ginger
1 small brown onion (80g), sliced thinly
1 teaspoon ground cumin
2 tablespoons mild curry powder
¹/₂ teaspoon ground cardamom
425g can tomatoes
1 teaspoon sugar
¹/₂ cup (125ml) water

1 Heat oil in medium saucepan; cook eggs, stirring occasionally, until eggs are well browned all over. Drain on absorbent paper; at this stage, eggs will have a crusty surface.

2 Reserve 1 tablespoon of the oil from saucepan; discard remaining oil. Reheat reserved oil in pan; cook seeds, covered, about 30 seconds or until seeds begin to crack.

3 Stir in garlic, ginger and onion; cook, stirring constantly, until onion is soft. Stir in cumin, curry powder, cardamom, undrained crushed tomatoes, sugar and the water.

4 Bring sauce to a boil. Add eggs; reduce heat. Cover; simmer about 5 minutes or until thickened slightly. Serve with rice, if desired.

serves 4

per serving 25.8g fat; 1343kJ
store Curried eggs can be made 1 day ahead and refrigerated, covered.

mexican-style
bread salad

PREPARATION TIME 15 MINUTES ▪ COOKING TIME 15 MINUTES

vegan

2 large pittas

1 tablespoon olive oil

2 medium egg tomatoes (150g)

2 large avocados (640g),
    sliced thinly

310g can corn kernels,
    rinsed, drained

300g can kidney beans,
    rinsed, drained

1/2 small cos lettuce

garlic and chilli dressing

1/4 cup (60ml) lemon juice

1/3 cup (80ml) olive oil

2 cloves garlic, crushed

1 teaspoon sambal oelek

2 tablespoons sweet chilli sauce

1 Brush both sides of pitta with oil; place on oven trays. Bake, uncovered, in moderately hot oven about 15 minutes or until crisp. Cool; break into pieces. *[Can be made 3 days ahead to this stage and stored in airtight container.]*

2 Cut tomatoes into wedges. Combine tomato, avocado, corn and beans in large bowl. Just before serving, add pitta pieces and garlic and chilli dressing; toss to combine. Place in lettuce-lined serving bowl.

garlic and chilli dressing Combine ingredients in screw-top jar; shake well. *[Can be made 1 day ahead to this stage and refrigerated, covered.]*

serves 6

per serving 33.7g fat; 1891kJ

zucchini and peanut
burgers

PREPARATION TIME 10 MINUTES ■ COOKING TIME 30 MINUTES

2 zucchini (200g), grated

½ cup (75g) roasted peanuts, chopped finely

2 eggs, beaten lightly

2 tablespoons finely chopped fresh parsley

½ cup (100g) cooked brown rice

½ cup (50g) stale breadcrumbs

plain flour

2 tablespoons vegetable oil

okra and tomato stew

1 tablespoon oil

1 medium onion (150g), sliced thinly

1 clove garlic, crushed

425g can tomatoes

12 (150g) okra

1 tablespoon finely chopped fresh parsley

1 Squeeze exces[...] [...]arsley, rice and bread[...]

2 Shape into six [...] [...]urgers until browned.

3 Serve with okr[...]

serves 6

per serving 14.6g fat; 1077kJ

[handwritten note: too much prep time! not good enough for effort it taked!]

okra and tomato stew Heat oil in medium saucepan; cook onion and garlic, stirring, until onion is soft. Add undrained crushed tomatoes, okra and parsley; simmer, covered, 20 minutes.

serves 6

per serving 3.3g fat; 224kJ

store Burgers can be prepared 3 hours ahead and refrigerated, covered; okra and tomato stew can be made 1 day ahead and refrigerated, covered.

burritos
with eggs and
pumpkin seed sauce

PREPARATION TIME 15 MINUTES ■ COOKING TIME 10 MINUTES

30g butter
8 eggs, beaten lightly
4 x 20cm warm tortillas
2 green onions, chopped finely
1 small fresh green chilli, chopped finely

pumpkin seed sauce
1/3 cup (50g) pepitas, roasted
1 green thai chilli, chopped finely
3/4 cup firmly packed fresh parsley sprigs
3/4 cup firmly packed fresh coriander sprigs
3/4 cup (180ml) vegetable stock

1 Heat butter in large saucepan; cook eggs, stirring gently, over low heat until creamy.

2 Top tortillas evenly with scrambled egg, onion, chilli and pumpkin seed sauce; roll up to enclose filling.

pumpkin seed sauce Blend or process ingredients until combined.
[Can be made 1 day ahead to this stage and refrigerated, covered.]

serves 4

per serving 25.9g fat; 1774kJ

white beans
in rich tomato sauce

PREPARATION TIME 5 MINUTES ■ COOKING TIME 15 MINUTES

vegan

1 tablespoon olive oil

**1 medium brown onion (150g),
chopped finely**

2 cloves garlic, crushed

415g can tomato puree

**2 x 400g cans cannellini beans,
rinsed, drained**

**1 tablespoon finely sliced fresh
flat-leaf parsley**

1 Heat oil in medium saucepan; cook onion and garlic, stirring, until onion is soft.

2 Stir in tomato puree and beans; simmer, uncovered, until thickened slightly. Stir in parsley.

serves 4

per serving 1g fat; 556kJ

store Recipe can be made 2 days ahead and refrigerated, covered; or frozen up to 3 months.

hot
tofu salad

PREPARATION TIME 15 MINUTES ■ COOKING TIME 10 MINUTES

1 medium red onion (170g)

3cm piece fresh ginger

2 teaspoons peanut oil

250g packet firm tofu, drained,
   chopped coarsely

1 small carrot (70g), sliced thinly

1 small red capsicum (150g),
   sliced thinly

100g broccoli, chopped coarsely

100g snow peas

1 trimmed stick celery (75g),
   sliced thinly

½ cup (125ml) vegetable stock

2 tablespoons oyster sauce

1 tablespoon salt-reduced
   soy sauce

1 Cut onion into thin wedges. Cut ginger into thin slices; cut slices into thin strips.

2 Heat oil in wok or large non-stick frying pan; cook onion, ginger and tofu until onion is soft and tofu browned lightly.

3 Stir in remaining ingredients; bring to a boil. Reduce heat; simmer, uncovered, about 5 minutes or until vegetables are tender.

serves 2

per serving 13.5g fat; 1249kJ

sesame zucchini fritters

vegan

PREPARATION TIME 15 MINUTES
COOKING TIME 15 MINUTES

4 medium zucchini (480g), grated coarsely

1 large potato (300g), grated coarsely

1/3 cup (50g) plain flour

1 tablespoon sesame oil

2 tablespoons sesame seeds

vegetable oil, for shallow-frying

1 Squeeze as much liquid as possible from combined zucchini and potato; pat dry with absorbent paper.

2 Combine vegetable mixture, flour, sesame oil and seeds in large bowl, mixing in flour well.

3 Shape 1/4-cup measures of mixture into patties. Shallow fry in hot oil, pressing each with an egg slide to flatten well. Cook until golden and crisp both sides. Drain on absorbent paper. Serve immediately with sea salt and freshly ground black pepper, if desired.

makes 12

per fritter 9.7g fat; 510kJ

fennel fritters

PREPARATION TIME 15 MINUTES
COOKING TIME 25 MINUTES

1 tablespoon finely chopped fresh fennel leaves

1 medium fennel bulb (500g), chopped finely

3 green onions, chopped finely

1 small carrot (70g), grated finely

2 eggs, beaten lightly

75g ricotta cheese

1/4 cup (35g) plain flour

2 teaspoons baking powder

vegetable oil, for shallow-frying

1 Combine fennel leaves and bulb, onion, carrot, egg, cheese, flour and baking powder in medium bowl; mix well.

2 Heat oil in large frying pan; shallow-fry heaped tablespoons of mixture until golden brown both sides and cooked through. Flatten slightly during cooking; drain on absorbent paper.

makes 16

per fritter 5.7g fat; 291kJ

chive potato patties

PREPARATION TIME 25 MINUTES
COOKING TIME 30 MINUTES

2 large old potatoes (600g), peeled, grated coarsely
¼ cup finely chopped fresh chives
½ cup (125ml) sour cream
2 tablespoons olive oil

1 Press potato between layers of absorbent paper to remove as much moisture as possible.

2 Combine potato, chives and sour cream in large bowl; mix well. Divide mixture into eight portions; shape into 8cm patties.

3 Heat oil in large frying pan; cook patties, in batches, until browned both sides. Place patties in a single layer on oven tray; bake, uncovered, in moderate oven about 20 minutes or until cooked through.

makes 8

per serving 15.2g fat; 779kJ

carrot and dill rosti

PREPARATION TIME 25 MINUTES
COOKING TIME 35 MINUTES

½ cup (125ml) light sour cream
1 teaspoon ground cumin
1 tablespoon finely chopped fresh dill
5 medium carrots (600g), grated
2 eggs, beaten lightly
⅓ cup (50g) plain flour

1 Combine sour cream, cumin and dill in small bowl.

2 Combine carrot, egg and flour in large bowl. Cook ¼-cup measures of carrot mixture, in batches, on heated oiled frying pan, until browned both sides and cooked through. Serve with sour cream mixture.

makes 8

per serving 4.7g fat; 384kJ

fritters

stir-fried mushrooms
and water spinach

8 dried shiitake mushrooms

1 tablespoon peanut oil

2 cloves garlic, crushed

1 teaspoon grated fresh ginger

400g oyster mushrooms, halved

400g button mushrooms, quartered

425g can straw mushrooms, drained

900g chinese water spinach, shredded

5 green onions, sliced thinly

1 tablespoon light soy sauce

1 tablespoon mild sweet chilli sauce

1 tablespoon oyster sauce

1 tablespoon rice vinegar

1 Place dried mushrooms in small heatproof bowl; cover with boiling water. Stand 20 minutes; drain. Discard stems; slice caps.

2 Heat oil in wok or large frying pan; stir-fry garlic, ginger and mushrooms 1 minute. Add spinach, onion and combined sauces and vinegar; stir-fry until spinach just wilts.

serves 6

per serving 4.5g fat; 454kJ

stir-fries

The ultimate in fast, fuss-free cooking, these creative stir-fries

combine the enticing flavours of Asia with your favourite

ingredients, in dishes such as lemon grass tofu on crisp noodles.

vegetable
chap-chai

PREPARATION TIME 25 MINUTES ■ COOKING TIME 15 MINUTES

1 tablespoon peanut oil

1 clove garlic, crushed

1 tablespoon grated fresh ginger

300g tat soi, trimmed

500g choy sum, chopped coarsely

400g baby bok choy,
chopped coarsely

450g chinese cabbage,
chopped coarsely

1 tablespoon soy sauce

½ cup (60ml) hoisin sauce

1 tablespoon plum sauce

2 teaspoons sambal oelek

1½ cups (120g) bean sprouts

1 Heat oil in wok or large frying pan; stir-fry garlic and ginger until fragrant.

2 Add tat soi, choy sum, bok choy, cabbage, combined sauces and sambal oelek; stir-fry until vegetables are just tender.

3 Add sprouts; stir-fry, tossing until sprouts just wilt.

serves 4

per serving 6.9g fat; 608kJ

satay vegetable
stir-fry

PREPARATION TIME 30 MINUTES (plus standing time) ■ COOKING TIME 25 MINUTES

375g firm tofu

1/4 cup (60ml) light soy sauce

1 teaspoon fish sauce

1 tablespoon sugar

1/2 teaspoon grated lime rind

2 teaspoons lime juice

2 tablespoons vegetable oil

1 medium red onion (170g), chopped finely

1 clove garlic, crushed

2 tablespoons finely chopped fresh lemon grass

1 teaspoon sambal oelek

1 teaspoon ground turmeric

1 teaspoon ground cumin

1 tablespoon paprika

1/3 cup (50g) unsalted roasted peanuts

1 medium carrot (120g)

1 medium green capsicum (200g)

3 small zucchini (270g)

3/4 medium cauliflower (750g), chopped coarsely

3/4 cup (180ml) coconut milk

1 cup (250ml) vegetable stock

1/3 cup (85g) smooth peanut butter

1 Wrap tofu in absorbent paper; squeeze out excess liquid. Cut tofu into 1.5cm x 4cm pieces; combine tofu, sauces, sugar, rind and juice in medium bowl. Cover; refrigerate overnight.

2 Heat oil in large saucepan; cook onion, garlic, lemon grass, sambal oelek, spices and peanuts, stirring, until onion is soft.

3 Cut carrot, capsicum and zucchini into matchstick-size pieces; add to pan with cauliflower, cocount milk, stock and peanut butter; bring to a boil. Reduce heat; simmer, covered, about 15 minutes or until vegetables are just tender.

4 Add tofu mixture; stir until heated through. Serve with rice, if desired.

serves 4

per serving 41g fat; 2448kJ

thyme and tofu
stir-fry

PREPARATION TIME 25 MINUTES ▓ COOKING TIME 15 MINUTES

vegan

350g cauliflower, chopped coarsely

350g broccoli, chopped coarsely

250g asparagus, sliced thickly

350g green beans, sliced thickly

3 medium carrots (360g), sliced thickly

¼ cup (60ml) olive oil

2 cloves garlic, crushed

1 tablespoon finely chopped fresh thyme

1 teaspoon cracked black pepper

375g firm tofu, drained, cubed

2 medium brown onions (300g), sliced thickly

250g button mushrooms, sliced thickly

½ cup (125ml) dry white wine

3 teaspoons cornflour

1 cup (250ml) vegetable stock

1 Cook cauliflower, broccoli, asparagus, beans and carrot in large saucepan of boiling water, uncovered, 2 minutes; drain. Rinse in cold water; drain.

2 Heat oil in wok or large frying pan. Stir-fry garlic, thyme, pepper and tofu until tofu is browned lightly; remove from wok.

3 Add onion and mushrooms to wok; stir-fry until onion is soft.

4 Add cauliflower mixture to wok with wine and blended cornflour and stock; stir-fry until sauce boils and thickens.

5 Add tofu mixture; stir gently until heated through.

serves 4

per serving 22g fat; 1684kJ

lemon grass tofu
on crisp noodles

PREPARATION TIME 15 MINUTES ■ COOKING TIME 20 MINUTES (plus standing time)

9 dried shiitake mushrooms

¼ cup (60ml) hoisin sauce

2 tablespoons tomato sauce

2 tablespoons fish sauce

**¼ cup finely chopped fresh
lemon grass**

3 red thai chillies, chopped finely

**1 large brown onion (200g),
chopped finely**

4 cloves garlic, crushed

**¼ cup finely chopped
fresh coriander**

**500g firm tofu, drained, cut into
3cm pieces**

vegetable oil, for deep-frying

100g thin rice stick noodles

2 teaspoons peanut oil

**1 medium red capsicum (200g),
sliced thinly**

100g snow peas, sliced coarsely

1 Place mushrooms in medium heatproof bowl; cover with boiling water. Stand 20 minutes; drain. Discard stems; slice caps.

2 Combine sauces, lemon grass, chilli, onion, garlic, coriander and tofu in large bowl; mix gently. Cover; stand at room temperature 30 minutes. *[Can be made 1 day ahead to this stage and refrigerated, covered.]*

3 Heat vegetable oil in large frying pan. Cook noodles until puffed; drain on absorbent paper.

4 Remove tofu from marinade; reserve marinade. Heat peanut oil in wok or large frying pan. Stir-fry tofu, in batches, until browned lightly; remove from wok.

5 Add mushrooms, capsicum, snow peas and reserved marinade to wok; stir-fry 3 minutes. Add tofu; stir-fry until hot.

6 Serve tofu mixture on noodles.

serves 4

per serving 21.5g fat; 1667kJ

chinese
mixed vegetables

PREPARATION TIME 20 MINUTES (plus standing time) ▓ COOKING TIME 10 MINUTES

3 dried cloud ear mushrooms

500g chinese broccoli

1 tablespoon peanut oil

2 medium carrots (240g), sliced thinly

2 cloves garlic, crushed

230g can water chestnuts, drained, sliced thinly

230g can bamboo shoots, drained

1 tablespoon oyster sauce

2 teaspoons satay sauce

1 teaspoon sesame oil

4 green onions, chopped finely

425g can baby corn, drained

2 cups (160g) bean sprouts

1 tablespoon finely chopped fresh coriander

1 Place mushrooms in small heatproof bowl. Cover with boiling water; stand 20 minutes. Drain; slice thinly. Discard tough ends from broccoli; chop broccoli coarsely.

2 Heat peanut oil in wok or large frying pan; stir-fry carrot until almost tender. Add mushrooms, garlic, water chestnuts, shoots, sauces, sesame oil, onion, corn and broccoli; stir-fry until broccoli is just tender.

3 Remove from heat. Add sprouts and coriander; toss until combined.

serves 4

per serving 7.6g fat; 789kJ

triple mushroom
omelette

PREPARATION TIME 15 MINUTES ▥ COOKING TIME 35 MINUTES (plus standing time)

12 dried shiitake mushrooms
3 dried cloud ear mushrooms
2 teaspoons peanut oil
6 green onions, sliced thinly
2 teaspoons grated fresh ginger
2 cloves garlic, crushed
1/2 medium red capsicum (100g), chopped finely
100g button mushrooms, sliced thinly
3/4 cup (60g) bean sprouts
1/4 cup (40g) pine nuts, toasted
90g snow peas, sliced thinly
1 tablespoon salt-reduced soy sauce
1 tablespoon oyster sauce
1 tablespoon water
10 eggs, beaten lightly
1/3 cup (80ml) water, extra

spicy sauce
2 red thai chillies, sliced thinly
1/4 cup (60ml) chinese barbecue sauce
1/3 cup (80ml) water

1 Place dried mushrooms in large heatproof bowl; cover with boiling water. Stand 20 minutes; drain. Discard stems; slice caps thinly.

2 Heat oil in wok or large frying pan; stir-fry onion, ginger, garlic, capsicum and mushrooms until capsicum is just soft. Add sprouts, pine nuts, snow peas and combined sauces and water, stirring until peas are just tender; keep warm.

3 Meanwhile, whisk eggs with the extra water in large bowl. Lightly oil 24cm heavy-base omelette pan; heat pan. Add 1/3 cup (80ml) of the egg mixture to pan; swirl pan to form a thin omelette over base. Cook until set; remove. Repeat with remaining egg mixture; cover omelettes with foil to keep warm. You will need eight omelettes.

4 Place 1/4 cup of the mushroom mixture on each omelette. Fold omelette over filling; fold over again. Serve omelettes topped with spicy sauce.

spicy sauce Combine ingredients in small saucepan; stir over heat until mixture boils. Reduce heat; simmer, uncovered, about 3 minutes or until thickened slightly.

serves 4

per serving 22.8g fat; 1442kJ

pepper-cream vegetables

PREPARATION TIME 30 MINUTES ■ COOKING TIME 15 MINUTES

1 tablespoon olive oil

**2 medium brown onions (300g),
    sliced thinly**

**2 medium carrots (240g),
    sliced thickly**

**4 baby eggplants (240g),
    sliced thickly**

250g button mushrooms, halved

**2 medium zucchini (240g),
    sliced thickly**

**1 medium red capsicum (200g),
    sliced thickly**

1 clove garlic, crushed

½ cup (125ml) vegetable stock

½ cup (125ml) cream

2 tablespoons cracked black pepper

1 Heat oil in wok or large frying pan. Stir-fry vegetables and garlic, in batches, until just tender; keep warm.

2 Add combined stock, cream and pepper to wok; stir until sauce thickens slightly.

3 Serve vegetables with sauce.

serves 4

per serving 19.2g fat; 1086kJ

warm beetroot and macadamia salad

PREPARATION TIME 35 MINUTES ■ COOKING TIME 15 MINUTES

8 medium beetroot (1.4kg)
40g ghee
2 small leeks (400g), sliced thickly
1 cup (150g) macadamias
1/4 cup (60ml) raspberry vinegar
1/4 cup (60ml) olive oil
1 clove garlic, crushed
250g baby rocket leaves
250g baby spinach leaves
150g goat cheese, crumbled

1 Boil, steam or microwave beetroot until tender; drain. Peel beetroot while warm; cut into wedges.

2 Meanwhile, heat ghee in wok or large frying pan; stir-fry leek and nuts until leek is soft and nuts are browned lightly.

3 Add beetroot, vinegar, oil and garlic to wok; stir-fry, tossing until beetroot is hot.

4 Remove from heat; toss rocket, spinach and cheese through beetroot mixture.

serves 6

per serving 39.6g fat; 2022kJ

stuffed
potatoes

PREPARATION TIME 5 MINUTES ■ COOKING TIME 1 HOUR

6 large old potatoes (1.8kg)
cooking-oil spray

1 Pierce skin of potatoes in several places using fork or skewer. Place potatoes on oven tray coated with cooking-oil spray.

2 Bake, uncovered, in moderately hot oven about 1 hour or until tender. Cut 5cm-deep cross in each potato; gently press sides to open cross.

herbed cottage cheese

PREPARATION TIME 15 MINUTES

250g low-fat cottage cheese
3 green onions, chopped finely
2 tablespoons grated parmesan cheese
2 tablespoons finely chopped fresh basil
1 tablespoon finely chopped fresh chives

Combine ingredients in medium bowl; spoon over hot potatoes.

serves 6
per serving 3g fat; 1110kJ

low-fat

Healthy eating is essential, so whether you're watching your weight or simply improving your health, these tasty recipes with less than 15.1g fat will help you feel great.

vegan spiced avocado
PREPARATION TIME 10 MINUTES

2 medium avocados (500g), chopped finely
1 teaspoon ground cumin
2 tablespoons finely chopped fresh coriander
2 tablespoons mild chilli sauce
2 teaspoons lemon juice

Combine ingredients in medium bowl; spoon over hot potatoes.

serves 6
per serving 13.7g fat; 1370kJ

minted salsa
PREPARATION TIME 5 MINUTES

2 tablespoons light cream cheese
2 medium tomatoes (380g), chopped finely
4 green onions, chopped finely
2 teaspoons shredded fresh mint

Top hot potatoes with cheese; spoon over combined remaining ingredients.

serves 6
per serving 1.5g fat; 916kJ

mushroom and leek
PREPARATION TIME 15 MINUTES ▪ COOKING TIME 10 MINUTES

1 tablespoon vegetable oil
1 medium leek (350g), sliced thinly
1 clove garlic, crushed
125g button mushrooms, sliced thinly
1 teaspoon powdered mustard
2 tablespoons cream

Heat oil in medium frying pan. Cook leek and garlic until leek is soft; add mushrooms. Cook, stirring until just soft; stir in mustard. Stir in cream; bring to a boil. Spoon over hot potatoes.

serves 6
per serving 6.5g fat; 1108kJ

white bean soup
with polenta croutons

PREPARATION TIME 20 MINUTES (plus refrigeration time) ■ COOKING TIME 35 MINUTES

1 tablespoon olive oil

2 small leeks (400g), sliced thinly

2 cloves garlic, crushed

2 trimmed sticks celery (150g), chopped finely

1.5 litres (6 cups) vegetable stock

1 tablespoon white wine vinegar

4 x 400g cans cannellini beans, drained, rinsed

½ cup (125ml) cream

2 teaspoons fresh thyme

polenta croutons

2 cups (500ml) water

½ cup (85g) polenta

¼ cup (20g) finely grated parmesan cheese

1 red thai chilli, seeded, chopped finely

1 Heat oil in large saucepan; cook leek and garlic, stirring, about 10 minutes or until leek is soft. Add celery; cook, stirring, 2 minutes.

2 Stir in stock, vinegar and half of the beans; bring to a boil. Reduce heat; simmer, covered, 10 minutes.

3 Blend or process bean mixture, in batches, until smooth. *[Can be made 1 day ahead to this stage and refrigerated, covered.]* Return bean mixture to cleaned pan.

4 Add remaining beans, cream and thyme to pan; stir over heat until soup is hot.

5 Just before serving, ladle soup into serving bowls; top with polenta croutons.

polenta croutons Grease 8cm x 26cm bar pan; line base and sides with baking paper. Bring the water to a boil in medium saucepan. Gradually stir in polenta; cook, stirring, over low heat about 5 minutes or until mixture is thick. Stir in cheese and chilli; spread polenta in prepared pan. Cover; refrigerate 3 hours or overnight. *[Can be made 1 day ahead to this stage and refrigerated, covered.]* Turn polenta onto board. Cut into 1cm slices; cut each slice into two triangles. Cook polenta pieces, in batches, on heated oiled grill plate (or grill or barbecue) until browned; drain on absorbent paper.

serves 6

per serving 15.1g fat; 1050kJ

buckwheat crepes
with spicy green bean filling

PREPARATION TIME 35 MINUTES ■ COOKING TIME 50 MINUTES (plus standing time)

½ cup (80g) wholemeal plain flour

½ cup (75g) buckwheat flour

1 egg, beaten lightly

1½ cups (375ml) milk

15g butter

100g oyster mushrooms

spicy green bean filling

300g green beans

2 teaspoons vegetable oil

1 medium brown onion (150g),
chopped finely

2 cloves garlic, crushed

1 small red capsicum (150g),
chopped finely

2 teaspoons garam masala

2 teaspoons ground cumin

½ teaspoon ground turmeric

¼ teaspoon chilli powder

5 medium tomatoes (950g), peeled,
chopped finely

1 tablespoon tomato paste

½ cup (100g) drained canned
corn kernels

½ cup (125ml) plain yogurt

1 Combine flours in medium bowl. Gradually stir in combined egg and milk; blend or process until smooth. Cover; stand 30 minutes.

2 Pour 2 to 3 tablespoons of the batter into heated oiled small heavy-base frying pan; cook until browned lightly underneath. Turn crepe; brown other side. Repeat with remaining batter. You will need 12 crepes for this recipe. *[Can be made 2 days ahead to this stage and refrigerated, covered, layered with greaseproof paper.]*

3 Divide spicy green bean filling between crepes; fold crepes into quarters.

4 Heat butter in small saucepan; cook mushrooms, stirring, over medium heat about 3 minutes or until tender. Serve with crepes.

spicy green bean filling Cut beans lengthways into strips; cut strips in half. Boil, steam or microwave until tender. Heat oil in medium saucepan; cook onion, garlic and capsicum, stirring, over medium heat about 2 minutes or until onion is soft. Add spices, tomato, paste and corn; bring to a boil. Reduce heat; simmer, covered, 10 minutes. Add beans; stir until hot. Remove from heat; gradually stir in yogurt.

serves 6

per serving 9g fat; 1082kJ
store Unfilled crepes can be frozen up to 2 months.

curried vegetable and
lentil flan

PREPARATION TIME 40 MINUTES (plus chilling time)   ▪ COOKING TIME 1 HOUR 15 MINUTES (plus cooling time)

cooking-oil spray

½ cup (100g) red lentils

1 cup (160g) wholemeal plain flour

¼ cup (35g) plain flour

60g low-fat cream cheese

1 egg white, beaten lightly

**2 teaspoons low-fat
milk, approximately**

2 eggs, beaten lightly

1 egg white, extra

¼ cup (60ml) low-fat milk, extra

⅓ cup (40g) grated low-fat cheese

filling

2 teaspoons vegetable oil

1 medium zucchini (120g), grated

1 medium carrot (120g), grated

1 medium parsnip (125g), grated

1 small leek (200g), sliced thinly

1 clove garlic, crushed

¼ teaspoon sambal oelek

3 teaspoons mild curry powder

2 teaspoons caraway seeds

**1 tablespoon coarsely chopped
fresh coriander**

1 Coat 24cm-round loose-base flan tin with cooking-oil spray.

2 Place lentils in large saucepan of boiling water; boil, uncovered, about 8 minutes or until just tender. Drain; cool.

3 Place flours in large bowl; rub in cream cheese. Add ½ cup of the lentils; reserve remaining lentils for filling. Add egg white and enough of the milk to make mixture cling together. Press dough into a ball; knead gently on floured surface until smooth. Cover; refrigerate 30 minutes.

4 Roll pastry between sheets of baking paper until large enough to line prepared tin; lift pastry into tin. Ease into side; trim edge. Lightly prick base with fork; refrigerate 30 minutes.

5 Cover pastry with baking paper; fill with dried beans or rice. Place on oven tray; bake, uncovered, in moderately hot oven 15 minutes. Remove paper and beans carefully from pastry case. Bake, uncovered, further 15 minutes or until browned; cool.

6 Spoon filling into prepared case. Pour over combined eggs, extra egg white and extra milk; sprinkle with grated cheese. Bake, uncovered, in moderately hot oven about 30 minutes or until set.

filling Heat oil in large saucepan; cook vegetables, garlic and sambal oelek, stirring, until vegetables are soft. Stir in curry powder and seeds; cook, stirring, until fragrant. Stir in reserved lentils and coriander.

serves 6

per serving 7.9g fat; 960kJ
store Flan can be made 1 day ahead and refrigerated, covered; uncooked pastry can be frozen up to 6 months.

ricotta gnocchi
with tomato sauce

PREPARATION TIME 35 MINUTES ■ COOKING TIME 10 MINUTES

960g silverbeet, trimmed

1¼ cups (250g) ricotta cheese

⅓ cup (30g) grated parmesan cheese

1 egg, beaten lightly

¼ teaspoon ground nutmeg

2 teaspoons plain flour

1 teaspoon grated parmesan cheese, extra

tomato sauce

425g can tomatoes

2 teaspoons sugar

1 teaspoon dried oregano leaves

1 Boil, steam or microwave silverbeet until tender; drain. Squeeze out excess liquid; chop finely.

2 Combine silverbeet in large bowl with ricotta, parmesan, egg and nutmeg; mix well. Roll into 12 balls; dust with flour.

3 Using spoon, gently place balls into large saucepan of boiling water. Reduce heat slightly; simmer about 2 minutes or until balls rise to surface.

4 Remove gnocchi using slotted spoon; drain. Serve immediately with sauce; sprinkle with extra parmesan.

tomato sauce   Blend or process undrained tomatoes until smooth; strain. Heat in medium saucepan with sugar and oregano.

serves 4

per serving   11.5g fat; 814kJ

rigatoni with fetta
and herbed tomatoes

PREPARATION TIME 25 MINUTES ■ COOKING TIME 15 MINUTES

375g rigatoni pasta

2 medium tomatoes (380g), seeded,
 sliced thinly

1 small red onion (100g),
 sliced thinly

¼ cup fresh flat-leaf parsley

90g low-fat fetta cheese

red capsicum dressing

1 small red capsicum (150g)

1 clove garlic, crushed

1 teaspoon coarsely chopped
 fresh thyme

1 tablespoon red wine vinegar

1 tablespoon lemon juice

⅓ cup (80ml) vegetable stock

1 Cook pasta in large saucepan of boiling water, uncovered, until just tender; drain.

2 Toss hot pasta with tomato, onion, parsley and red capsicum dressing in large bowl; sprinkle with crumbled cheese.

red capsicum dressing Quarter capsicum; remove and discard seeds and membranes. Roast under grill or in very hot oven, skin-side up, until skin blisters and blackens. Cover capsicum pieces in plastic or paper for 5 minutes. Peel away skin; chop coarsely. Blend or process capsicum and remaining ingredients until smooth; sieve into small bowl. *[Can be made 1 day ahead and refrigerated, covered.]*

serves 4

per serving 4.6g fat; 1688kJ

felafel rolls
with tabbouleh

PREPARATION TIME 55 MINUTES ■ COOKING TIME 40 MINUTES (plus standing time)

250g frozen broad beans

310g can chickpeas, rinsed, drained

2 cloves garlic, crushed

6 green onions, chopped finely

1 teaspoon ground cumin

1/2 teaspoon ground coriander

1/4 cup finely chopped fresh parsley

1/4 cup finely chopped fresh mint

2 tablespoons polenta, approximately

cooking-oil spray

1 small green cucumber (130g)

8 cos lettuce leaves

**400g packet wholemeal
    lebanese bread**

tabbouleh

2 tablespoons burghul

2/3 cup finely chopped fresh parsley

2 green onions, chopped finely

**1 medium tomato (130g),
    chopped finely**

1 teaspoon lemon juice

2 teaspoons olive oil

yogurt sauce

1 cup (250ml) low-fat yogurt

1 clove garlic, crushed

2 teaspoons lemon juice

1 teaspoon low-salt soy sauce

**2 teaspoons finely chopped
    fresh mint**

1 Place beans in medium bowl; cover with boiling water. Stand 5 minutes; drain. Remove and discard outer skins; drain on absorbent paper.

2 Blend or process beans, chickpeas, garlic, onion, cumin, coriander and herbs until combined. Shape level teaspoons of mixture into patties; roll in polenta. Place on oven tray coated with cooking-oil spray; coat felafel with cooking-oil spray.

3 Bake, uncovered, in hot oven about 40 minutes or until browned.

4 Using vegetable peeler, cut cucumber into strips lengthways. Divide lettuce, tabbouleh, cucumber, felafel and yogurt sauce between bread; fold over filling.

tabbouleh Place burghul in small bowl; cover with boiling water. Stand 10 minutes; drain. Blot dry with absorbent paper. Combine burghul with remaining ingredients in large bowl; mix well.

yogurt sauce Combine ingredients in medium bowl; mix well.

serves 4

per serving 6.9g fat; 1920kJ
store Felafel can be made 1 day ahead and refrigerated, covered.

fresh tomato and
fennel soup

PREPARATION TIME 20 MINUTES ■ COOKING TIME 40 MINUTES

2 medium fennel bulbs (1kg)

60g butter

2 medium brown onions (300g), chopped coarsely

2 cloves garlic, quartered

2kg egg tomatoes, quartered

2 cloves garlic, crushed, extra

3 cups (750ml) vegetable stock

1 Trim fennel; reserve 1/2 cup of the fine uppermost leaves. Chop a third of the fennel finely; reserve. Chop remaining fennel coarsely.

2 Melt two-thirds of the butter in large saucepan; cook coarsely chopped fennel, onion and garlic, stirring, until onion is soft. Add tomato; cook, uncovered, stirring occasionally, about 30 minutes or until tomato is very soft and pulpy.

3 Blend or process soup mixture, in batches, until smooth. Pass mixture through food mill or fine sieve; return to pan.

4 Heat remaining butter in small frying pan; cook extra garlic and finely chopped fennel, stirring, until fennel is just soft and golden brown. Add to soup with stock; bring to a boil. *[Can be made 1 day ahead to this stage and refrigerated, covered.]*

5 Simmer about 5 minutes or until soup is hot. Just before serving, stir in finely chopped reserved fennel leaves.

serves 6

per serving 8.9g fat; 799kJ
store Soup may be frozen up to 6 months.
tip 1 teaspoon of pernod can be added to each bowl of soup as a substitute for fennel leaves, if preferred.

honey mustard-glazed
kumara

PREPARATION TIME 15 MINUTES ▪ COOKING TIME 35 MINUTES

2 large kumara (1kg), peeled
6 baby brown onions (150g), halved
½ cup (125ml) honey
2 tablespoons balsamic vinegar
2 tablespoons seeded mustard
1 tablespoon water
1 tablespoon peanut oil
1 tablespoon grated fresh ginger
50g baby rocket leaves

1 Slice kumara into 1cm rounds. Place kumara and onion in large bowl; toss with combined honey, vinegar, mustard, water, oil and ginger. Drain vegetables; reserve honey-mustard mixture.

2 Place vegetables on wire rack over foil-covered oven tray. Bake, uncovered, in moderately hot oven about 35 minutes, brushing frequently during cooking with honey-mustard mixture, until vegetables are browned lightly. Serve with rocket.

serves 4

per serving 5.2g fat; 1542kJ

lentil patties
with yogurt mint sauce

PREPARATION TIME 20 MINUTES ■ COOKING TIME 30 MINUTES (plus cooling time)

1/2 **cup (100g) red lentils**

1/2 **trimmed stick celery (35g), chopped finely**

1 **small carrot (70g), chopped finely**

2 **cups (500ml) water**

1/2 **teaspoon ground coriander**

1/2 **teaspoon ground cumin**

2 **cups (140g) stale breadcrumbs**

2 **tablespoons plain flour**

1 **egg white, beaten lightly**

1 **tablespoon finely chopped fresh parsley**

1 **tablespoon monounsaturated or polyunsaturated oil**

yogurt mint sauce

1/2 **cup (125ml) low-fat yogurt**

1 **tablespoon finely chopped fresh mint**

1 **small clove garlic, crushed**

1 **teaspoon lemon juice**

1 Combine lentils, celery, carrot, the water, coriander and cumin in large saucepan. Bring to a boil; reduce heat. Simmer, covered, about 20 minutes or until mixture thickens; cool.

2 Stir in half of the breadcrumbs. Shape mixture into four patties; toss in flour. Dip in egg white; dip in combined remaining breadcrumbs and parsley. *[Can be made 1 day ahead to this stage and refrigerated, covered.]*

3 Heat oil in large non-stick frying pan; cook patties until well browned both sides. Drain on absorbent paper; serve with yogurt mint sauce and green leaf salad, if desired.

yogurt mint sauce Combine ingredients in small bowl; mix well.

serves 2

per serving 14.3g fat; 2433kJ
store Uncooked patties and yogurt mint sauce can be made 1 day ahead and refrigerated, covered, separately. Uncooked patties can be frozen up to 6 months.

cannellini beans with
polenta

PREPARATION TIME 15 MINUTES (plus standing time) ■ COOKING TIME 35 MINUTES

1 litre (4 cups) water

2 cups (340g) polenta

1 cup (80g) finely grated parmesan cheese

1 tablespoon olive oil

1 medium brown onion (150g), sliced thinly

1 clove garlic, crushed

2 x 400g cans tomatoes

¾ cup (180ml) vegetable stock

2 tablespoons tomato paste

1 red thai chilli, seeded, chopped finely

2 x 400g cans cannellini beans, rinsed, drained

500g spinach, trimmed, chopped coarsely

1 tablespoon finely shredded fresh basil

1 Oil 23cm-square slab cake pan. Bring the water to a boil in large saucepan; gradually whisk in polenta. Reduce heat; simmer, whisking, about 5 minutes or until mixture thickens. Stir in cheese.

2 Smooth polenta mixture in prepared pan. Cover; refrigerate about 3 hours or until firm. *[Can be made 1 day ahead to this stage and refrigerated, covered.]*

3 Turn polenta onto board; cut polenta in half. Cut each half into quarters; cut each quarter in half diagonally.

4 Heat oil in medium saucepan; cook onion and garlic, stirring, until onion is soft. Add undrained crushed tomatoes, stock, paste and chilli; bring to a boil. Reduce heat; simmer, uncovered, about 5 minutes or until thickened slightly.

5 Add beans, spinach and basil; cook, uncovered, until spinach is wilted and beans are hot.

6 Just before serving, cook polenta triangles, in batches, on large heated dry grill plate (or grill or barbecue) until browned both sides; drain on absorbent paper. Serve with tomato bean mixture and mesclun tossed in a balsamic vinaigrette, if desired.

serves 8

per serving 7.4g fat; 1214kJ

tips Any kind of dried beans can be substituted for canned beans, if preferred. Soak beans overnight. Boil until tender; drain.

Use patience when spreading polenta into prepared pan; it tends to move and slip but can eventually be worked into corners of pan.

vegetable
moussaka

PREPARATION TIME 10 MINUTES ■ COOKING TIME 1 HOUR 15 MINUTES (plus cooling time)

**1 large eggplant (500g),
  sliced thickly**

**2 large tomatoes (500g),
  chopped finely**

1 teaspoon sugar

2 teaspoons butter

1 tablespoon plain flour

1 cup (250ml) skim milk

**2 tablespoons finely grated
  parmesan cheese**

**2 tablespoons finely chopped
  fresh basil**

1 Place eggplant in single layer on oven tray. Bake, uncovered, in moderately hot oven 15 minutes; turn. Bake further 15 minutes or until browned lightly; cool 10 minutes.

2 Combine tomato and sugar in small saucepan; cook, stirring occasionally, about 30 minutes or until tomato is soft and liquid almost evaporates.

3 Meanwhile, melt butter in small saucepan; add flour. Cook, stirring, 1 minute. Gradually add milk; stir over medium heat until sauce boils and thickens. Stir in half of the cheese and half of the basil. Stir remaining basil through tomato mixture.

4 Spread a third of the tomato mixture, eggplant and cheese sauce in two 2-cup (500ml) ovenproof dishes; repeat with two more layers. Sprinkle with remaining cheese.

5 Bake, uncovered, in moderate oven, about 15 minutes or until moussaka is browned lightly.

serves 2

per serving 7.4g fat; 937kJ
store Moussaka can be prepared 3 hours ahead and refrigerated, covered.

spinach and pumpkin curry

PREPARATION TIME 20 MINUTES ▧ COOKING TIME 20 MINUTES

1 tablespoon ghee
2 medium brown onions (300g), sliced thinly
2 cloves garlic, crushed
1 teaspoon grated fresh ginger
2 green thai chillies, seeded, sliced thinly
1 teaspoon ground coriander
1 teaspoon ground cumin
1 teaspoon black mustard seeds
$1/2$ teaspoon ground turmeric
1kg pumpkin, peeled, cut into 3cm pieces
$1^1/2$ cups (375ml) vegetable stock
150g spinach, chopped coarsely
$1/3$ cup loosely packed fresh coriander
1 tablespoon flaked almonds, toasted

1 Heat ghee in large saucepan; cook onion, stirring, until browned.

2 Add garlic, ginger, chilli and spices; stir over heat until fragrant.

3 Add pumpkin and stock; simmer, covered, about 15 minutes or until pumpkin is tender. Add spinach and coriander; tossing, until spinach is just wilted.

4 Just before serving, sprinkle nuts over curry. Serve with steamed rice, if desired.

serves 4

per serving 7.4g fat; 686kJ (excluding rice)
store Curry can be made 1 day ahead and refrigerated, covered.

vegetable risotto

PREPARATION TIME 10 MINUTES (plus standing time) ■ COOKING TIME 45 MINUTES

1 small eggplant (230g), chopped finely

coarse cooking salt

2 teaspoons olive oil

1 small brown onion (80g), chopped finely

1 clove garlic, crushed

3/4 cup (150g) brown rice

3/4 cup (180ml) vegetable stock

2 cups (500ml) water

2 medium zucchini (240g)

2 medium tomatoes (380g), peeled, chopped finely

125g mushrooms, sliced thinly

1/4 cup (20g) coarsely grated parmesan cheese

1 tablespoon fresh oregano

1 Place eggplant in colander; sprinkle with salt. Stand 30 minutes; rinse well under cold water. Pat dry with absorbent paper.

2 Heat oil in large saucepan; cook onion and garlic, until soft. Add rice, stock and the water; bring to a boil. Reduce heat; simmer, covered, about 30 minutes or until rice is tender and almost all the liquid is absorbed.

3 Using vegetable peeler, cut zucchini into thin strips, lengthways.

4 Stir eggplant, zucchini, tomato and mushrooms into rice; cook about 3 minutes or until vegetables soften. Stir in half of the cheese and oregano; serve risotto sprinkled with remaining cheese.

serves 2

per serving 11.2g fat; 1923kJ

stir-fried
mushrooms, beans and bok choy

PREPARATION TIME 10 MINUTES ■ COOKING TIME 10 MINUTES

vegan

1 teaspoon sesame oil

1 tablespoon vegetable oil

500g baby bok choy, quartered

1 small chinese cabbage (400g), shredded coarsely

450g broccoli, chopped finely

100g shiitake mushrooms

150g oyster mushrooms

310g can red kidney beans, rinsed, drained

1/3 cup (80ml) hoisin sauce

1/4 cup (60ml) lime juice

1/4 cup (60ml) orange juice

1 Heat oils in wok or large non-stick frying pan; stir-fry bok choy and cabbage until just wilted.

2 Add broccoli, mushrooms, beans, sauce and juices; cook, covered, about 3 minutes or until broccoli is tender.

serves 4

per serving 8.1g fat; 932kJ

mushroom, spinach and lemon
risotto

PREPARATION TIME 5 MINUTES ▦ COOKING TIME 30 MINUTES (plus standing time)

1 tablespoon olive oil

2 medium brown onions (300g), chopped finely

3 cloves garlic, crushed

1 tablespoon finely grated lemon rind

300g button mushrooms, halved

2 cups (400g) arborio rice

1.5 litres (6 cups) vegetable stock

1 cup (250ml) dry white wine

300g baby spinach leaves

2 tablespoons coarsely chopped fresh lemon thyme

1 Heat oil in large saucepan; cook onion, garlic, rind and mushrooms, stirring, until mushrooms are browned lightly.

2 Add rice, stock and wine; bring to a boil. Reduce heat; simmer, covered, 15 minutes, stirring halfway during cooking.

3 Remove from heat. Cover; stand 10 minutes. Gently stir in spinach and lemon thyme. Serve with shaved parmesan, if desired.

serves 4

per serving 1.6g fat; 1916kJ

rice, grains and pulses

Whether you're cooking a pilaf, risotto or hotpot,
incorporate tasty ingredients such as artichoke, lemon
and tomato to make every meal a tantalising delight.

couscous
with orange and pumpkin

PREPARATION TIME 20 MINUTES (plus standing time) ■ COOKING TIME 20 MINUTES

vegan

1½ cups (250g) couscous

3 cups (750ml) water

750g pumpkin, chopped coarsely

1 tablespoon olive oil

2 medium brown onions (300g), chopped finely

2 cloves garlic, crushed

2 teaspoons grated orange rind

½ cup (125ml) orange juice

⅓ cup (50g) coarsely chopped dried apricots

½ cup (80g) dry roasted almonds, chopped coarsely

¼ cup (15g) thinly sliced fresh mint

1 Combine couscous and the water in medium bowl; stand about 15 minutes or until the water is absorbed.

2 Meanwhile, boil, steam or microwave pumpkin until tender; drain.

3 Heat oil in large frying pan; cook onion and garlic, stirring over medium heat about 3 minutes or until tender and browned lightly.

4 Add rind, juice, apricot, couscous and pumpkin; stir until heated through. Serve sprinkled with nuts and mint.

serves 4

per serving 16g fat; 1092kJ

tip Substitute roasted pumpkin for boiled pumpkin, if preferred.

rice and fetta
roasted capsicums

PREPARATION TIME 15 MINUTES ■ COOKING TIME 30 MINUTES

2 large red capsicums (700g), halved, seeded

2 teaspoons olive oil

1 small brown onion (80g), chopped finely

2 cloves garlic, crushed

¾ cup (150g) calrose rice

1 cup (250ml) vegetable stock

1 cup (250ml) water

1 tablespoon lemon juice

300g spinach, trimmed

2 tablespoons finely chopped fresh mint

1 tablespoon pine nuts, toasted

1 tablespoon dried currants

50g fetta cheese, crumbled

1 Place capsicum in medium baking dish; bake, uncovered, in hot oven 15 minutes.

2 Meanwhile, heat oil in medium saucepan; cook onion and garlic, stirring, until onion is soft. Add rice, stock, the water and juice; simmer, covered, stirring occasionally, about 15 minutes or until rice is just tender. Add spinach, mint, nuts and currants; stir until combined.

3 Spoon rice mixture into capsicum halves; top with cheese. Bake, uncovered, in hot oven about 15 minutes or until heated through.

serves 4

per serving 8.2g fat; 1160kJ

lentil balls
with tomatoes and rocket

PREPARATION TIME 30 MINUTES ■ COOKING TIME 25 MINUTES

vegan

1 cup (200g) red lentils

2 tablespoons olive oil

2 medium zucchini (240g), grated coarsely

1 small brown onion (80g), chopped finely

1 red thai chilli, chopped finely

1 cup (70g) stale breadcrumbs

1/4 cup (35g) white sesame seeds, toasted

1 tablespoon finely chopped fresh coriander

1/3 cup (35g) packaged breadcrumbs

vegetable oil for deep-frying

5 medium egg tomatoes (375g), quartered

2 cloves garlic, crushed

120g rocket

2 tablespoons shredded fresh mint

2 tablespoons shredded fresh basil

1/4 cup (60ml) white wine vinegar

1 Add lentils to large saucepan of boiling water; boil, uncovered, about 8 minutes or until just tender. Drain; press out liquid.

2 Meanwhile, heat half of the olive oil in wok or large frying pan; stir-fry zucchini, onion and chilli until onion is just soft.

3 Combine lentils, zucchini mixture, stale breadcrumbs, seeds and coriander in medium bowl. Roll teaspoonfuls of the mixture into balls; toss in packaged breadcrumbs.

4 Heat vegetable oil in large frying pan. Deep-fry balls, in batches, until browned; drain on absorbent paper.

5 Heat remaining olive oil in wok; stir-fry tomato and garlic. Return lentil balls to wok; stir until hot.

6 Remove wok from heat. Add rocket, mint, basil and vinegar; toss to combine.

serves 4

per serving 16.5g fat; 1924kJ

mixed mushroom
risotto

PREPARATION TIME 10 MINUTES ■ COOKING TIME 50 MINUTES

80g butter

2 tablespoons olive oil

100g swiss brown mushrooms, sliced thinly

200g flat mushrooms, sliced thinly

1.5 litres (6 cups) hot vegetable stock

1 medium brown onion (150g), chopped finely

2 cloves garlic, crushed

2 cups (400g) arborio rice

2/3 cup (160ml) dry white wine

1/2 cup (40g) grated parmesan cheese

40g butter, chopped, extra

1/4 cup finely chopped flat-leaf parsley

1 Heat half of the butter and oil in large saucepan. Cook mushrooms, stirring over medium heat until soft. Remove from pan; cover.

2 Meanwhile, bring stock to a boil in large saucepan. Cover; keep hot.

3 Heat remaining butter and oil in pan; cook onion and garlic, stirring, until onion is soft. Add rice; cook, stirring, until rice is coated in butter mixture. Stir in wine; simmer, uncovered, until wine is absorbed.

4 Add 1/2 cup (125ml) of the stock; cook, stirring, over low heat until liquid is absorbed. Continue adding stock, in 1/2-cup (125ml) batches, stirring, until liquid is absorbed after each addition. [*This will take about 35 minutes or until rice is just tender.*]

5 Remove from heat; stir in cheese, extra butter, mushrooms and parsley.

6 Serve immediately; top with shaved parmesan, if desired.

serves 4

per serving 30.2g fat; 2990kJ

barley and vegetable
hotpot

PREPARATION TIME 25 MINUTES ■ COOKING TIME 1 HOUR 5 MINUTES

vegan

1 cup (200g) pearl barley

1 tablespoon olive oil

2 medium brown onions (300g), chopped finely

2 medium carrots (350g), chopped coarsely

2 trimmed sticks celery (150g), chopped coarsely

2 cloves garlic, crushed

2 cobs corn (500g)

2 large parsnips (360g), chopped coarsely

2 cups (500ml) vegetable stock

1 cup (250ml) water

500g pumpkin, chopped coarsely

1/3 cup finely chopped flat-leaf parsley

2 1/2 tablespoons miso paste

1 Place barley in large saucepan. Cover with water; bring to a boil. Reduce heat to low; cook, uncovered, 30 minutes or until tender. Drain; reserve. *[Can be made 1 day ahead to this stage and refrigerated, covered.]*

2 Heat oil in large saucepan; cook onion, carrot, celery and garlic over medium heat, stirring occasionally, about 10 minutes or until vegetables are almost tender.

3 Remove corn kernels from cobs. Add corn kernels, parsnip, stock and the water to pan; cook, uncovered, over medium heat for 15 minutes or until almost tender. Add pumpkin; cook further 5 minutes or until all vegetables are tender.

4 Stir in barley and parsley; cook until heated through. *[Can be made 1 day ahead to this stage and refrigerated, covered.]*

5 Stir 1 teaspoon of miso into each cup of heated hotpot.

serves 6

per serving 6g fat; 1239kJ

artichokes
with wild rice seasoning

PREPARATION TIME 1 HOUR ▦ COOKING TIME 55 MINUTES

**8 medium fresh globe
artichokes (1.6kg)**

1½ cups (375ml) water

1 cup (250ml) dry white wine

½ cup (125ml) olive oil

2 tablespoons lemon juice

2 cloves garlic, crushed

6 sprigs fresh thyme

wild rice seasoning

**1 cup (200g) wild rice/brown
rice blend**

2 tablespoons olive oil

**1 medium brown onion (150g),
chopped finely**

2 cloves garlic, crushed

**½ cup (70g) drained sun-dried
capsicums, chopped finely**

**⅓ cup finely chopped
fresh oregano**

¼ cup (40g) pine nuts, toasted

2 teaspoons olive paste

1 tablespoon drained baby capers

⅓ cup (25g) grated romano cheese

rocket salad

1 medium radicchio lettuce

50g rocket leaves

**1 cup firmly packed fresh
flat-leaf parsley**

1½ tablespoons balsamic vinegar

⅓ cup (80ml) olive oil

1 Remove tough outer leaves from artichokes; trim tips of remaining leaves. Pull away some inside leaves; scoop out coarse centre with spoon. Peel stem; trim to 5cm.

2 Combine the water, wine, oil, juice, garlic and thyme in large saucepan; bring to a boil. Add artichokes; reduce heat. Simmer, covered, about 20 minutes or until tender. Drain artichokes; discard cooking liquid. *[Can be made 1 day ahead to this stage and refrigerated, covered.]*

3 Cut artichokes in half lengthways; fill with wild rice seasoning.

4 Serve with rocket salad.

wild rice seasoning Place rice in large saucepan of boiling water. Boil, uncovered, about 35 minutes or until tender; drain. Rinse under cold water; drain. Heat oil in large saucepan; cook onion and garlic, stirring, until soft. Stir in rice and remaining ingredients. *[Can be made 1 day ahead to this stage and refrigerated, covered.]*

rocket salad Combine torn radicchio leaves, rocket and parsley in large bowl; drizzle with combined vinegar and oil.

serves 4

per serving 69.9g fat; 3825kJ

soya patties
with lemon and herb yogurt

PREPARATION TIME 20 MINUTES ■ COOKING TIME 25 MINUTES

1 tablespoon olive oil

1 medium red onion (170g),
  chopped finely

1 medium red capsicum (200g),
  chopped finely

2 cloves garlic, crushed

3 cups (210g) stale breadcrumbs

2 x 300g cans soy beans,
  rinsed, drained

2 eggs, beaten lightly

1/2 cup finely chopped fresh parsley

2 teaspoons grated lemon rind

3/4 cup (60g) grated
  parmesan cheese

1/3 cup (50g) pine nuts, toasted

lemon and herb yogurt

200g yogurt

1 clove garlic, crushed

1 tablespoon lemon juice

2 tablespoons finely chopped
  fresh parsley

2 tablespoons finely chopped
  fresh chives

1 Heat oil in medium saucepan; cook onion, capsicum and garlic, stirring, until onion is soft.

2 Process breadcrumbs, beans, egg, parsley, rind, half of the cheese and onion mixture until just combined; stir in nuts.

3 Shape 1/3-cup measures of the mixture into patties. Place patties on oiled baking tray; sprinkle with remaining cheese.

4 Bake in hot oven about 20 minutes, turning halfway during cooking, or until browned lightly.

5 Serve patties with lemon and herb yogurt and steamed asparagus and rocket leaves, if desired.

lemon and herb yogurt Combine ingredients in small bowl.

serves 4

per serving 30g fat; 2416kJ
store Recipe can be made 1 day ahead and refrigerated, covered. Uncooked patties can be frozen up to 4 months.

leek and saffron
barley

PREPARATION TIME 10 MINUTES ▪ COOKING TIME 35 MINUTES

vegan

1 tablespoon extra virgin olive oil

2 medium leeks (700g), sliced thinly

3 cloves garlic, crushed

1 cup (200g) pearl barley, rinsed

3 cups (750ml) vegetable stock

pinch saffron threads

**1/3 cup finely chopped fresh
     flat-leaf parsley**

1 Heat oil in large saucepan; cook leek and garlic, stirring, over medium heat for 2 minutes, or until softened.

2 Add barley, stock and saffron; bring to a boil. Reduce heat to low; cook, covered, about 30 minutes or until barley softens, stirring occasionally. Stir in parsley.

serves 4

per serving 5g fat; 1000kJ

leek and rice flan
with sesame mushrooms

PREPARATION TIME 30 MINUTES (plus refrigeration time) ▥ COOKING TIME 1 HOUR 15 MINUTES (plus cooling time)

¾ cup (150g) basmati rice

½ small brown onion (40g),
  chopped finely

¼ cup (20g) grated
  parmesan cheese

1 tablespoon finely chopped
  fresh coriander

1 egg, beaten lightly

½ teaspoon dried chilli flakes

leek filling

60g butter

3 large leeks (1.5kg), shredded

1½ tablespoons grated fresh ginger

¼ cup finely chopped
  fresh coriander

3 eggs, beaten lightly

1 cup (250ml) cream

sesame mushrooms

2 teaspoons sesame oil

1 tablespoon vegetable oil

4 cloves garlic, crushed

¼ cup (35g) white sesame seeds

600g swiss brown mushrooms

2 tablespoons soy sauce

2 tablespoons sake

1 Grease deep 19cm-square cake pan. Line base and two opposite sides with foil; grease foil well.

2 Place rice in large saucepan of boiling water. Boil, uncovered, until tender; drain well.

3 Combine rice and remaining ingredients in large bowl; mix well. Press mixture evenly over base and halfway up sides of prepared pan. Place pan on oven tray; refrigerate 30 minutes.

4 Pour leek filling into rice crust. Bake, uncovered, in moderately hot oven about 45 minutes or until browned and firm.

5 Serve with sesame mushrooms.

leek filling Heat butter in medium saucepan. Cook leek, ginger and coriander, stirring, until leek is soft; cool. Combine leek mixture, egg and cream in large bowl; mix well.

sesame mushrooms Heat oils in large saucepan; cook garlic and seeds, stirring, until seeds are browned lightly. Add remaining ingredients; cook, stirring, until mushrooms are soft.

serves 6

per serving 39.8g fat; 2265kJ
store Flan can be made 1 day ahead and refrigerated, covered.

grilled eggplants, tomato and
chickpeas

PREPARATION TIME 20 MINUTES ■ COOKING TIME 1 HOUR

vegan

**2 medium eggplants (600g),
sliced thickly**

2 tablespoons olive oil

10 spring onions (250g), trimmed

2 cloves garlic, crushed

**3 trimmed sticks celery (225g),
sliced thinly**

**2 x 310g cans chickpeas,
rinsed, drained**

**4 large tomatoes (1kg), peeled,
chopped finely**

¼ cup finely chopped fresh parsley

**¼ cup finely chopped
fresh oregano**

1 tablespoon tomato paste

150g sugar snap peas, trimmed

1 Place eggplant slices on greased oven tray; brush lightly with about half of the oil. Grill until browned both sides.

2 Heat remaining oil in 3-litre (12-cup) flameproof casserole dish; cook onions, stirring, until browned lightly.

3 Stir in eggplant, garlic, celery, chickpeas, tomato and herbs. Cook, covered, in moderate oven about 45 minutes or until vegetables are tender.

4 Remove from oven; stir in paste and peas.

serves 4

per serving 12.2g fat; 1145kJ
store Recipe can be made 1 day ahead and refrigerated, covered.

black bean, rice and
vegetable pilaf

PREPARATION TIME 10 MINUTES ■ COOKING TIME 55 MINUTES

½ cup (100g) mexican black
  turtle beans

1 large red onion (300g)

30g butter

1 teaspoon cumin seeds

1 teaspoon coriander seeds

1 cinnamon stick

6 cardamom pods

3 cloves

1 teaspoon ground turmeric

1 teaspoon garam masala

1 medium carrot (120g), sliced thinly

1½ cups (300g) long-grain rice

1½ cups (375ml) vegetable stock

1½ cups (375ml) water

1 medium green capsicum (200g),
  chopped coarsely

1 Place beans in medium saucepan of boiling water. Boil, uncovered, about 40 minutes or until tender; drain.

2 Cut onion into wedges. Heat butter in large saucepan; cook onion and spices, stirring, about 1 minute or until fragrant. Add carrot and rice, stir until combined. Add stock and the water; simmer, covered, 8 minutes. Add beans and capsicum; simmer, covered, about 2 minutes or until rice is tender and liquid is absorbed.

serves 4

per serving 7.7g fat; 1679kJ

sun-dried tomato
quiche

PREPARATION TIME 30 MINUTES (plus refrigeration time) ■ COOKING TIME 1 HOUR

½ cup (100g) cottage cheese

100g butter, softened

1⅓ cups (200g) plain flour

1 tablespoon olive oil

1 medium brown onion (150g), sliced thinly

¼ cup (35g) drained sun-dried tomatoes, chopped finely

¼ cup finely shredded fresh basil

¾ cup (60g) grated gruyere cheese

¼ cup (20g) grated parmesan cheese

3 eggs, beaten lightly

¾ cup (180ml) cream

¼ cup (30g) grated tasty cheese

1 Combine cottage cheese and butter in large bowl; stir in flour. Press dough into a ball; knead, gently, on floured surface until smooth. Cover; refrigerate 30 minutes.

2 Roll dough on floured surface until large enough to line 24cm-round flan tin. Ease pastry into tin; trim edge.

3 Place tin on oven tray; cover pastry with baking paper. Fill with dried beans or rice; bake, uncovered, in moderately hot oven 10 minutes. Remove paper and beans; bake further 10 minutes or until browned.

4 Heat oil in medium saucepan. Cook onion until soft; drain on absorbent paper.

5 Spread onion, tomato, basil, gruyere and parmesan into pastry case. Top with combined egg and cream; sprinkle with tasty cheese.

6 Bake, uncovered, in moderate oven about 35 minutes or until set.

bacon option Sprinkle non-vegetarians' portions with crumbled cooked bacon.

serves 6

per serving 40.7g fat; 2281kJ

store Recipe can be made 1 day ahead and refrigerated, covered.

almost vegetarian

Whether you're a meat-eater with vegetarian children, or a committed vegetarian with a carnivorous partner, this is the chapter for you. The recipes are vegetarian, but each includes a meat option, which will quickly and easily transform the vegetarian dish into something suitable for everyone.

mexican broad bean **burgers**

PREPARATION TIME 30 MINUTES (plus refrigeration time) ■ COOKING TIME 1 HOUR 20 MINUTES

1 tablespoon olive oil

2 medium red onions (340g),
  sliced thinly

6 hamburger buns

225g vegetarian refried beans

1 medium avocado (250g),
  sliced thinly

½ cup (125ml) sour cream

½ cup (125ml) mild chilli sauce

broad bean patties

½ cup (100g) pearl barley

1kg frozen broad beans

1 medium white onion (150g), grated

1¾ cups (120g) stale breadcrumbs

2 eggs

1 tablespoon milk

100g cheese-flavoured corn chips,
  crushed finely

salsa

1 medium tomato (190g),
  chopped finely

1 small red onion (100g),
  chopped finely

1 tablespoon coarsely chopped
  fresh coriander

1 tablespoon lime juice

1 teaspoon sugar

1 Heat oil in small frying pan; cook onion, stirring, until soft.

2 Split and toast buns. Fill buns with broad bean patties, heated beans, avocado, salsa, onion, sour cream and sauce.

broad bean patties Place barley in large saucepan of boiling water. Boil, uncovered, about 40 minutes or until tender; drain. Pour boiling water over beans in medium heatproof bowl. Stand 2 minutes; drain. Remove skins from beans; blend or process beans until smooth. Combine barley, bean puree, onion, 1 cup of the breadcrumbs and one of the eggs in large bowl; mix well. Shape mixture into six patties; dip in combined remaining egg and milk. Press on combined corn chips and remaining breadcrumbs. Place patties on greased oven tray. Cover; refrigerate 1 hour. Bake, uncovered, in moderately hot oven about 25 minutes or until firm. *[Can be made 1 day ahead to this stage and refrigerated, covered.]*

salsa Combine ingredients in small bowl; mix well.

bacon option Place a halved cooked bacon rasher on top of heated beans and continue layering as above.

makes 6

per serving 28.6g fat; 2825kJ

tacos with kidney beans

PREPARATION TIME 15 MINUTES ■ COOKING TIME 20 MINUTES

vegan

1 tablespoon olive oil

1 medium brown onion (150g),
chopped coarsely

1 clove garlic, crushed

1 thai red chilli, seeded,
chopped finely

2 medium tomatoes (380g),
chopped finely

2 tablespoons tomato paste

1 tablespoon taco seasoning

1 cup (250g) vegetarian
refried beans

420g can red kidney beans,
drained, rinsed

2 tablespoons coarsely chopped
fresh coriander

12 taco shells

1 medium avocado (250g),
chopped finely

4 green onions, chopped finely

1 small red capsicum (150g),
chopped finely

1 Heat oil in medium saucepan; cook brown onion, garlic and chilli, stirring, until onion is soft.

2 Stir in tomato, paste and seasoning; simmer, uncovered, 10 minutes.

3 Add beans; simmer about 5 minutes or until hot. Stir in coriander. *[Can be made 1 day ahead to this stage and refrigerated, covered.]*

4 Prepare taco shells as instructed on packet.

5 Fill taco shells with bean mixture; top with combined avocado, green onion and capsicum.

beef option Stir cooked beef mince into non-vegetarians' portions.

makes 12

per serving 8.2g fat; 653kJ
store Filling can be frozen up to 1 month.

tomato and mushroom
calzone

PREPARATION TIME 45 MINUTES (plus standing time) ■ COOKING TIME 1 HOUR (plus cooling time)

vegan **2 teaspoons (7g) dried yeast**

1/2 teaspoon sugar

1/2 cup (125ml) warm water

1 cup (150g) plain flour

1/2 cup (75g) polenta

1/2 teaspoon salt

2 tablespoons olive oil

1 tablespoon polenta, extra

tomato sauce

1 tablespoon olive oil

**1 medium brown onion (150g),
chopped finely**

2 cloves garlic, crushed

425g can tomatoes

1/4 cup (70g) tomato paste

1 teaspoon sugar

**1 tablespoon finely chopped
fresh oregano**

**2 teaspoons finely chopped
fresh thyme**

mushroom filling

1 tablespoon olive oil

**150g flat mushrooms,
chopped finely**

12 drained artichoke hearts, halved

**2 tablespoons drained capers,
chopped finely**

**1 tablespoon finely chopped
fresh dill**

1 Lightly oil 30cm pizza pan.

2 Combine yeast, sugar and the water in medium bowl; stand about 10 minutes or until frothy.

3 Combine flour, polenta and salt in large bowl; stir in yeast mixture and oil. Mix to a firm dough.

4 Knead dough on floured surface about 8 minutes or until smooth and elastic. Roll dough until large enough to fit prepared pan.

5 Place dough on pan; spread with tomato sauce, leaving 3cm border.

6 Spoon mushroom filling over half of the dough; brush border with water. Fold over other half to enclose filling; fold edge to seal. Sprinkle with extra polenta.

7 Stand calzone in warm place about 10 minutes or until risen. Bake in moderately hot oven about 35 minutes or until browned.

tomato sauce Heat oil in large saucepan; cook onion and garlic, stirring, until onion is soft. Add undrained crushed tomatoes and remaining ingredients. Simmer, uncovered, about 15 minutes or until mixture is thickened; cool.

mushroom filling Heat oil in large saucepan; cook mushrooms, stirring, until browned lightly and liquid has evaporated. Stir in artichokes, capers and dill.

fish option Sprinkle non-vegetarians' portions with chopped smoked salmon before folding dough over to enclose filling.

serves 4

per serving 20g fat; 1881kJ

store Tomato sauce and mushroom filling can be made a day ahead and refrigerated, covered, separately; tomato sauce suitable to freeze.

nutty rice
with figs and apricots

PREPARATION TIME 20 MINUTES ■ COOKING TIME 15 MINUTES (plus cooling time)

vegan

1 teaspoon cumin seeds

**2 tablespoons sunflower
  seed kernels**

2 tablespoons pepitas

1 cup (200g) white rice

1 cup (200g) brown rice

**½ cup (75g) dried apricots,
  sliced thinly**

**½ cup (95g) dried figs,
  chopped finely**

**1 cup (150g) unsalted
  roasted cashews**

⅓ cup (50g) pine nuts, toasted

⅔ cup (110g) almond kernels

dressing

¼ cup (60ml) red wine vinegar

½ cup (125ml) olive oil

**2 teaspoons finely chopped
  fresh oregano**

**2 teaspoons coarsely chopped
  fresh chives**

1 Place seeds, kernels and pepitas in dry medium saucepan; stir over heat until seeds begin to crack.

2 Place white and brown rice in separate medium saucepans of boiling water; boil, uncovered, until tender. Drain; cool. *[Can be made 1 day ahead to this stage and refrigerated, covered.]*

3 Combine seed mixture, rice and remaining ingredients in large bowl. Add dressing; mix well.

dressing Combine ingredients in screw-top jar; shake well.

fish option Grill white fish cutlets. Cool; flake into pieces. Top rice salad with fish.

serves 4

per serving 78.3g fat; 5158kJ

cheese polenta
with mushroom rosemary sauce

PREPARATION TIME 30 MINUTES ■ COOKING TIME 35 MINUTES (plus cooling time)

1 cup (250ml) milk

1½ cups (375ml) vegetable stock

1½ cups (375ml) water

1 cup (150g) polenta

1 cup (80g) coarsely grated
   parmesan cheese

plain flour

vegetable oil, for deep-frying

mushroom rosemary sauce

100g butter

300g oyster mushrooms, halved

400g swiss brown mushrooms

300g button mushrooms, halved

2 tablespoons fresh rosemary

¼ cup (60ml) dry white wine

½ cup (120g) sour cream

2 teaspoons worcestershire sauce

2 teaspoons dijon mustard

1 Grease 19cm x 29cm rectangular slice pan; line base and sides with baking paper.

2 Combine milk, stock and the water in large saucepan; bring to a boil. Add polenta; stir over heat about 10 minutes or until polenta is thick. Stir in cheese.

3 Press mixture into prepared pan; cool. Cover; refrigerate until cold. *[Can be made 1 day ahead to this stage and refrigerated, covered.]*

4 Turn out polenta; cut into triangles. Toss triangles in flour; shake away excess flour.

5 Heat oil in large frying pan; deep-fry polenta until browned; drain on absorbent paper.

6 Serve with mushroom rosemary sauce.

mushroom rosemary sauce Heat butter in large saucepan; cook mushrooms and rosemary, stirring, 2 minutes. Add remaining ingredients; cook, stirring, until mushrooms are soft.

ham option Sprinkle with finely chopped ham.

serves 4

per serving 59.3g fat; 3294kJ
store Fried polenta can be frozen up to 3 months.

cheese pasties
with tomato sauce

PREPARATION TIME 50 MINUTES (plus refrigeration time) ▓ COOKING TIME 35 MINUTES

1½ cups (240g) wholemeal
    plain flour

½ cup (75g) plain flour

½ cup (75g) self-raising flour

185g butter

2 teaspoons lemon juice

¼ cup (60ml) water, approximately

ricotta cheese filling

¾ cup (150g) ricotta cheese

¼ cup (20g) grated
    parmesan cheese

1 egg, beaten lightly

1 medium tomato (190g),
    chopped finely

60g button mushrooms, sliced thinly

1 teaspoon finely chopped
    fresh basil

2 tablespoons finely chopped
    fresh parsley

tomato sauce

15g butter

1 medium brown onion (150g),
    chopped finely

1 clove garlic, crushed

425g can tomatoes

200g button mushrooms,
    sliced thinly

2 teaspoons raw sugar

1 tablespoon finely chopped
    fresh basil

1 Process flours and butter until just crumbly; gradually stir in juice and enough of the water to mix to a firm dough.

2 Knead dough on floured surface until smooth; cover with plastic wrap. Refrigerate 30 minutes. *[Can be made 3 hours ahead to this stage and refrigerated, covered.]*

3 Roll dough out on floured surface to a 35cm x 45cm rectangle; cut into 12 rounds using 10cm cutter.

4 Place 1 tablespoon of the ricotta cheese filling in centre of each round. Lightly brush edges with water; press edges together to seal.

5 Place pasties on oiled oven tray; prick top of pasties using fork. Bake, uncovered, in hot oven, about 25 minutes or until browned lightly. Serve with tomato sauce.

ricotta cheese filling Combine ingredients in medium bowl.

tomato sauce Heat butter in small saucepan; cook onion and garlic, stirring, over medium heat about 2 minutes or until onion is soft. Blend or process undrained tomatoes; add to onion mixture. Stir in mushrooms, sugar and basil; bring to a boil. Reduce heat; simmer, uncovered, about 5 minutes or until sauce thickens slightly.

ham option Add a little finely chopped ham to ricotta cheese filling.

serves 4

per serving 50.4g fat; 3523kJ

burghul and wild rice
salad

PREPARATION TIME 40 MINUTES (plus standing time) ■ COOKING TIME 55 MINUTES

vegan

2 cups (320g) burghul

²⁄₃ cup (120g) wild rice

2 medium red capsicums (400g)

200g baby yellow squash, quartered

4 green onions, chopped finely

²⁄₃ cup (70g) pecans or walnuts

2 tablespoons finely chopped fresh parsley

dressing

²⁄₃ cup (160ml) olive oil

2 tablespoons lemon juice

1 clove garlic, crushed

¹⁄₂ teaspoon seasoned pepper

1 Place burghul in medium heatproof bowl; cover with boiling water. Stand 15 minutes; drain. Rinse under cold water; drain. Blot dry with absorbent paper.

2 Add rice to large saucepan of boiling water. Boil, uncovered, about 35 minutes or until rice is tender; drain. Rinse under cold water; drain.

3 Quarter capsicums; remove seeds and membranes. Grill capsicum, skin-side up, until skin blisters and blackens; cover with plastic or paper 5 minutes. Peel away skin; cut capsicum into thick strips.

4 Add squash to medium saucepan of boiling water; reduce heat. Simmer, uncovered, until squash is tender; drain. Rinse under cold water; drain.

5 Combine burghul, rice, capsicum, squash, onion, nuts and parsley in large bowl. Drizzle dressing over salad.

dressing Combine ingredients in screw-top jar; shake well.

quail option Cut quails into quarters; cook on heated oiled grill plate (or grill or barbecue) until tender. Top salad with quail.

serves 4

per serving 50.9g fat; 3366kJ
store Salad can be made 3 hours ahead and refrigerated, covered.

polenta
with sun-dried tomato dressing

PREPARATION TIME 25 MINUTES (plus refrigeration time) ■ COOKING TIME 30 MINUTES

3¼ cups (810ml) vegetable stock

1⅔ cups (410ml) skim milk

1½ cups (250g) polenta

⅓ cup (40g) grated reduced-fat cheddar cheese

2 cloves garlic, crushed

2 teaspoons olive oil

1 large leek (500g), sliced thickly

1 tablespoon sugar

sun-dried tomato dressing

cooking-oil spray

2 small brown onions (160g), chopped finely

2 cloves garlic, crushed

¼ cup (60ml) balsamic vinegar

1½ cups (90g) sun-dried tomatoes

2½ cups (625ml) vegetable stock

1 Bring stock and milk to a boil in large saucepan; stir in polenta. Reduce heat; simmer, stirring, about 10 minutes or until thick. Stir in cheese and garlic; spread into greased 23cm square cake pan; refrigerate 30 minutes or until firm. [Can be made 1 day ahead to this stage and refrigerated, covered.]

2 Heat oil in medium saucepan; cook leek, stirring, until soft. Add sugar; stir until browned.

3 Cut polenta into eight 7cm rounds; cook in heated oiled large saucepan until browned.

4 Serve polenta with leek mixture, sun-dried tomato dressing and rocket leaves, if desired.

sun-dried tomato dressing Coat medium non-stick saucepan with cooking-oil spray; cook onion and garlic, stirring, until tender. Stir in remaining ingredients; simmer, uncovered, about 10 minutes or until mixture is thickened slightly. [Can be made 1 day ahead to this stage and refrigerated, covered.]

beef option Grill beef eye fillet steaks; slice. Place on polenta and top with sun-dried tomato dressing.

serves 4

per serving 8.7g fat; 1846kJ
store Polenta can be frozen up to 3 months.

hot spinach
cheesecake

PREPARATION TIME 25 MINUTES (plus refrigeration time)
COOKING TIME 1 HOUR 20 MINUTES (plus standing time)

60g butter
1 cup (100g) finely crushed cheese biscuit crumbs
1/4 cup (20g) grated parmesan cheese

spinach filling
600g spinach, trimmed
1 medium brown onion (150g), chopped finely
250g cream cheese
125g fetta cheese
1 cup (250ml) sour cream
4 eggs, beaten lightly

1 Melt butter in medium saucepan. Add biscuit crumbs; mix well. Press evenly over base of greased 20cm springform pan; refrigerate, covered, 30 minutes.

2 Stand biscuit base on oven tray and pour spinach filling over. Bake, uncovered, in moderately slow oven about 1¼ hours or until golden brown and set. Sprinkle with cheese; stand 10 minutes before cutting.

spinach filling Boil, steam or microwave spinach until just tender; drain. Press excess liquid from spinach; chop spinach coarsely. Cook onion in small frying pan, stirring constantly, until onion is soft. Beat cheeses in small bowl with electric mixer until smooth. Add sour cream and egg; beat until combined. Transfer to large bowl; stir in spinach and onion.

bacon option Sprinkle with chopped cooked bacon rashers.

serves 8

per serving 38.5g fat; 1827kJ
store Cheesecake can be made 1 day ahead and refrigerated, covered.

gnocchi
with caramelised pumpkin and sage sauce

PREPARATION TIME 25 MINUTES ■ COOKING TIME 50 MINUTES

500g pumpkin

¼ cup (60ml) vegetable stock

1 large leek (500g), sliced thinly

1 tablespoon brown sugar

1½ cups (375ml) water

2 teaspoons finely chopped fresh sage

½ cup (125ml) low-fat evaporated milk

1kg fresh potato gnocchi

1 Chop pumpkin into 1cm cubes. Place pumpkin in oiled baking dish; bake, uncovered, in hot oven about 30 minutes or until pumpkin is tender.

2 Bring stock to a boil in large saucepan. Add leek; cook, stirring, until leek softens.

3 Add pumpkin and sugar; cook, stirring, about 10 minutes or until pumpkin is caramelised.

4 Stir in the water, sage and milk; blend or process pumpkin mixture, in batches, until smooth.

5 Return pumpkin sauce to pan; stir over heat until hot.

6 Meanwhile, place gnocchi in large saucepan of boiling water. Cook, uncovered, until just tender; drain. Toss hot gnocchi through hot pumpkin sauce.

prosciutto option Sprinkle with chopped cooked prosciutto.

serves 4

per serving 3.7g fat; 1932kJ

tandoori potato and pumpkin
pizza

PREPARATION TIME 25 MINUTES ■ COOKING TIME 1 HOUR 20 MINUTES

1 cup (200g) yellow split peas

1 litre (4 cups) water

2 tablespoons coarsely chopped fresh coriander

400g pumpkin, sliced thinly

4 medium potatoes (800g), sliced thinly

2 teaspoons peanut oil

2 medium brown onions (300g), sliced thinly

1 tablespoon grated fresh ginger

2 x 335g pizza bases

60g baby rocket leaves

400g low-fat yogurt

2 tablespoons finely chopped fresh mint

tandoori spice mix

2 teaspoons ground cumin

2 teaspoons ground turmeric

2 teaspoons sweet paprika

2 teaspoons ground coriander

1/4 teaspoon cayenne pepper

2 teaspoons peanut oil

1 Rinse split peas under cold running water until water runs clear; place split peas and the water in medium saucepan. Bring to a boil; reduce heat. Simmer, uncovered, about 45 minutes or until tender; drain. Blend or process until smooth; transfer to large bowl. Stir in coriander. *[Can be made 1 day ahead to this stage and refrigerated, covered.]*

2 Combine pumpkin, potato and tandoori spice mix in baking dish; mix well. Bake, uncovered, in hot oven about 15 minutes or until just tender.

3 Meanwhile, heat oil in small saucepan; cook onion and ginger, stirring, until onion is soft.

4 Place pizza bases on oven trays. Spread with split pea mixture; top with onion and potato mixtures. Bake, uncovered, in very hot oven about 15 minutes or until bases are crisp.

5 Top pizzas with rocket and combined yogurt and mint.

tandoori spice mix Combine ingredients in small bowl; mix well.

lamb option Cook lamb fillets in heated large non-stick frying pan until browned all over; slice thinly. Place on top of non-vegetarians' portions of pizza; cook as above.

serves 6

per serving 9.9g fat; 2608kJ

spicy vegetables
with chickpeas

PREPARATION TIME 20 MINUTES (plus standing time) ■ COOKING TIME 40 MINUTES

vegan

2 large eggplants (1kg)

coarse cooking salt

⅓ cup (80ml) olive oil

**1 medium leek (350g),
chopped coarsely**

2 cloves garlic, crushed

1 teaspoon ground cumin

1 teaspoon ground cardamom

1 teaspoon ground turmeric

1 teaspoon ground sweet paprika

½ teaspoon ground cinnamon

2 x 425g cans tomatoes

425g can chickpeas, drained

**3 small zucchini (270g),
sliced thickly**

150g green beans, halved

350g baby yellow squash, halved

200g baby carrots, halved

**½ cup (75g) pistachios, toasted,
chopped coarsely**

⅓ cup finely chopped fresh parsley

¼ cup finely chopped fresh mint

**¼ cup finely chopped
fresh coriander**

1½ cups (375ml) vegetable stock

300g spinach, trimmed, shredded

1 Cut eggplants into 1cm slices; place in colander. Sprinkle with salt; stand 30 minutes. Rinse slices under cold running water; drain. Pat dry with absorbent paper. Brush slices with half of the oil; place in single layer on oven trays. Grill both sides until browned lightly; drain on absorbent paper. Cut slices in half.

2 Heat remaining oil in medium saucepan; cook leek, garlic and spices, stirring, until leek is soft. Add undrained crushed tomatoes, chickpeas, vegetables, nuts, herbs and stock; simmer, covered, until vegetables are tender.

3 Add spinach and eggplant to vegetable mixture; simmer, covered, about 5 minutes or until spinach wilts.

lamb option Add cooked, sliced lamb fillets to non-vegetarians' portions at end of cooking.

serves 6

per serving 21.3g fat; 1437kJ
store Recipe can be made 1 day ahead and refrigerated, covered.

thai-style green vegetable curry

PREPARATION TIME 20 MINUTES ■ COOKING TIME 20 MINUTES

cooking-oil spray

2 tablespoons finely chopped lemon grass

4 kaffir lime leaves, shredded

1 medium leek (350g), sliced thickly

2 tablespoons Thai-style green curry paste

2 x 375ml cans evaporated low-fat milk

1 litre (4 cups) vegetable stock

2 tablespoons soy sauce

4 small green zucchini (360g), chopped coarsely

300g green beans, halved

½ small chinese cabbage (200g), chopped coarsely

330g choy sum, chopped coarsely

200g baby spinach leaves

1½ teaspoons coconut essence

2 tablespoons lime juice

¼ cup coarsely chopped fresh coriander

1 Coat large saucepan with cooking-oil spray; cook lemon grass, lime leaves and leek, stirring, until leek is soft. Add paste; stir until fragrant.

2 Stir in milk, stock and sauce; simmer, uncovered, 5 minutes or until thickened slightly.

3 Add vegetables; simmer, uncovered, until vegetables are just tender. Stir in essence, juice and coriander.

fish option Steam boneless firm white fish fillets; cool, flake into pieces. Top curry with fish.

serves 4

per serving 10.6g fat; 891kJ

kumara **risotto**

PREPARATION TIME 25 MINUTES ■ COOKING TIME 1 HOUR 10 MINUTES

**2 medium kumara (800g),
  chopped finely**

1 tablespoon olive oil

2 teaspoons sugar

1 litre (4 cups) vegetable stock

**1 medium onion (150g),
  chopped finely**

2 cloves garlic, crushed

2 cups (400g) arborio rice

½ cup (125ml) dry white wine

250g rocket, trimmed

¼ cup (60ml) thickened light cream

**1 tablespoon finely chopped
  fresh chives**

1 Boil, steam or microwave kumara until almost tender; drain. Place kumara in large baking dish; drizzle with half of the oil. Sprinkle with sugar; bake, uncovered, in hot oven about 30 minutes or until browned and tender.

2 Meanwhile, bring stock to a boil in large saucepan; reduce heat. Cover; simmer.

3 Heat remaining oil in large saucepan; cook onion, stirring, until soft. Add garlic and rice; cook, stirring, about 2 minutes or until well combined.

4 Add wine; cook, stirring, over low heat until liquid is absorbed. Stir in 1 cup (250ml) hot stock; cook, stirring, over low heat, until liquid is absorbed. Continue adding stock in 1 cup batches, stirring, until absorbed after each addition. Total cooking time should be about 35 minutes or until rice is just tender.

5 Gently stir in rocket, cream and kumara; sprinkle with chives. Serve with parmesan cheese flakes and extra whole chives, if desired.

chicken option Cook single chicken breast fillets in lightly oiled non-stick frying pan until browned both sides and cooked through. Slice chicken; stir through non-vegetarians' portions.

serves 4

per serving 10.8g fat; 2709kJ

swede and kumara
bake

PREPARATION TIME 20 MINUTES ■ COOKING TIME 1 HOUR 30 MINUTES

500g swedes, sliced thickly

250g kumara, sliced thickly

**1 medium brown onion (150g),
  sliced thinly**

¾ cup (90g) grated cheddar cheese

**¼ cup (20g) grated
  parmesan cheese**

**2 tablespoons coarsely chopped
  fresh dill**

2 teaspoons cracked black pepper

½ cup (125ml) cream

1 Oil 2.5 litre (10-cup) shallow ovenproof dish. Layer half of the swede, kumara
   and onion in prepared dish; sprinkle with half of the combined cheeses, dill
   and pepper. Repeat with remaining swede, kumara and onion. Pour cream
   over top of vegetables; top with remaining cheese mixture.

2 Bake, covered, in moderate oven 1 hour. Uncover; bake further 30 minutes or
   until top is browned and vegetables are tender.

serves 6

per serving 15.3g fat; 876kJ
store Recipe can be made 1 day ahead and refrigerated, covered.

casseroles and bakes

Enhance the flavour of your favourite vegetables
in these nutritious, hearty meals including potato and
cauliflower gratin and garlic, vegetable and rice casserole.

garlic, vegetable and rice
casserole

PREPARATION TIME 25 MINUTES ■ COOKING TIME 1 HOUR 10 MINUTES

vegan

1 bulb garlic (70g)

2 tablespoons olive oil

1 medium brown onion (150g),
   sliced thinly

1 medium red capsicum (200g),
   sliced thinly

1 medium green capsicum (200g),
   sliced thinly

4 medium tomatoes (760g), peeled,
   sliced thinly

125g green beans, trimmed, halved

2 small baby eggplants (120g),
   sliced thinly

¼ cup (35g) dried currants

1 teaspoon ground sweet paprika

1½ cups (300g) long-grain
   white rice

3 cups (750ml) boiling
   vegetable stock

1 Place unpeeled garlic on oven tray; brush with a little of the oil. Bake, uncovered, in moderately hot oven about 30 minutes or until slightly soft.

2 Heat remaining oil in large flameproof baking dish; cook onion, capsicums, tomato, beans and eggplant, stirring, about 10 minutes or until vegetables are just soft. Stir in currants and paprika.

3 Sprinkle rice over vegetables; pour stock over rice. Place garlic in centre of mixture; bake, uncovered, in moderately hot oven about 30 minutes, stirring halfway during cooking, or until rice is just tender.

serves 4

per serving 11.3g fat; 1983kJ

ratatouille

PREPARATION TIME 20 MINUTES (plus standing time) ■ COOKING TIME 20 MINUTES

vegan

2 medium zucchini (240g), cut into 3cm pieces

1 large eggplant (500g), cut into 3cm pieces

coarse cooking salt

1 medium red capsicum (200g)

1 medium yellow capsicum (200g)

1 medium green capsicum (200g)

1/4 cup (60ml) olive oil

1 medium brown onion (150g), chopped coarsely

2 cloves garlic, crushed

6 large egg tomatoes (540g), peeled, quartered

1/4 cup firmly packed torn fresh basil

1 Place zucchini and eggplant in sieve or colander; sprinkle with salt. Place large plate on top. Weigh down with heavy can; stand 30 minutes.

2 Meanwhile, halve capsicums; discard seeds and membranes. Cut capsicums into 3cm-square pieces.

3 Rinse zucchini and eggplant under cold running water; pat dry with absorbent paper.

4 Heat 1 tablespoon of the oil in large heavy-base frying pan. Cook onion and garlic, stirring, until onion is soft; remove from pan.

5 Heat half of the remaining oil in pan; cook zucchini and eggplant, in batches, until just tender. Add remaining oil to pan. Cook capsicums, in batches, until just tender; remove from pan.

6 Place onion mixture and tomato in pan; bring to a boil. Reduce heat; simmer, uncovered, about 15 minutes or until sauce thickens slightly. Add zucchini, eggplant, capsicums and basil; heat briefly, occasionally stirring gently, until ratatouille is hot.

serves 4

per serving 15.5g fat; 904kJ

store Ratatouille can be made 1 day ahead and refrigerated, covered.

eggplant timbales
with roasted tomato sauce

PREPARATION TIME 25 MINUTES (plus standing time) ■ COOKING TIME 1 HOUR

1 large eggplant (500g), sliced thinly

coarse cooking salt

100g somen noodles

1 tablespoon olive oil

1 medium leek (350g), sliced thinly

**1 medium carrot (120g),
  grated coarsely**

**1 medium zucchini (120g),
  grated coarsely**

4 eggs, beaten lightly

**1 tablespoon finely chopped
  fresh oregano**

1/4 cup (60ml) cream

1/2 cup (100g) crumbled fetta cheese

**1/4 cup (20g) coarsely grated
  parmesan cheese**

roasted tomato sauce

3 small tomatoes (390g), halved

1 teaspoon salt

2 cloves garlic, crushed

1/4 cup (60ml) olive oil

1/2 teaspoon sugar

1 tablespoon red wine vinegar

1 Place eggplant on wire rack. Sprinkle with salt; stand 30 minutes. Rinse under cold water; pat dry with absorbent paper. Cook eggplant on heated oiled grill plate (or grill or barbecue) until browned lightly both sides.

2 Meanwhile, cook noodles in large saucepan of boiling water, uncovered, until just tender; drain. Heat oil in medium saucepan; cook leek, carrot and zucchini, stirring, until vegetables are soft. Transfer to large bowl; stir in noodles, egg, oregano, cream and cheeses.

3 Overlap four eggplant slices over base and side of each of four 1 1/4-cup (310ml) ovenproof dishes; extend eggplant slices slightly above edge of dishes.

4 Divide noodle mixture among prepared dishes; fold eggplant over filling. Top timbales with remaining eggplant slices; press down firmly.

5 Cover timbales with foil; place on oven tray.

6 Bake, uncovered, in moderate oven about 35 minutes or until firm. Serve timbales with roasted tomato sauce.

roasted tomato sauce Place tomato in baking dish; sprinkle with salt and combined garlic and 1 tablespoon of the oil. Bake, uncovered, in hot oven about 20 minutes or until soft; cool. Blend or process tomato, remaining oil, sugar and vinegar until pureed. Press through fine sieve into small saucepan; discard pulp. Stir over medium heat until heated through. *[Can be made 1 day ahead to this stage and refrigerated, covered.]*

serves 4

per serving 38.6g fat; 2237kJ
tip Because of their supple texture when cooked, somen noodles work particularly well as the major ingredient in the timbale filling. A similarly fine, dried thin wheat noodle can be substituted, if preferred.

nut loaf
with tomato sauce

PREPARATION TIME 25 MINUTES ■ COOKING TIME 55 MINUTES

1 tablespoon vegetable oil

**1 medium brown onion (150g),
chopped finely**

**1 medium green capsicum (200g),
chopped finely**

**1 medium tomato (190g),
chopped finely**

**1 cup (150g) unsalted
roasted cashews**

1 cup (160g) blanched almonds

1 medium carrot (120g), grated

1 cup cooked brown rice

¾ cup (90g) grated cheddar cheese

1 egg, beaten lightly

tomato sauce

1 tablespoon vegetable oil

**6 medium tomatoes (1.2kg),
chopped finely**

¼ cup (60ml) water

1 Lightly oil 14cm x 21cm loaf pan; line base with greaseproof paper.

2 Heat oil in small frying pan. Cook onion, capsicum and tomato, stirring, over low heat about 4 minutes or until capsicum is tender; cool.

3 Blend or process cashews and almonds until chopped finely. Combine onion mixture, nuts, carrot, rice, cheese and egg in large bowl; mix well.

4 Press mixture evenly into prepared pan; bake, uncovered, in moderate oven about 40 minutes or until browned lightly. Serve with tomato sauce.

tomato sauce Heat oil in medium saucepan; cook tomato, stirring, over low heat 10 minutes. Blend or process tomato and the water until smooth. Strain over medium saucepan; reheat before serving.

serves 4

per serving 68g fat; 3655kJ

store Loaf and sauce can be made 1 day ahead and refrigerated, covered separately. You will need to cook about ⅓ cup (50g) brown rice for this recipe.

casserole

PREPARATION TIME 10 MINUTES (plus standing time) ■ COOKING TIME 1 HOUR

½ cup (100g) dried red
   kidney beans

½ cup (100g) dried chickpeas

2 teaspoons butter

1 medium red onion (170g),
   sliced thinly

1 medium carrot (120g),
   chopped coarsely

1 small red capsicum (150g),
   chopped finely

1 clove garlic, crushed

1 red thai chilli, chopped finely

1 teaspoon ground cumin

½ teaspoon ground cinnamon

½ teaspoon ground nutmeg

410g can tomatoes

½ cup (125ml) vegetable stock

2 teaspoons tomato paste

½ cup (100g) canned corn
   kernels, drained

2 teaspoons finely chopped
   fresh parsley

1 Cover beans and chickpeas with water in medium bowl. Stand overnight; drain. [Can be made 1 day ahead to this stage and refrigerated, covered.]

2 Heat butter in large saucepan; cook onion, carrot, capsicum, garlic and chilli until onion is soft.

3 Stir in spices; cook further 1 minute. Stir in beans and chickpeas, undrained crushed tomatoes, stock and paste. Bring to a boil; reduce heat. Simmer, covered, about 45 minutes, stirring occasionally, or until beans and chickpeas are tender.

4 Stir in corn; simmer further 5 minutes. Just before serving sprinkle with parsley.

serves 2

per serving 9.4g fat; 1899kJ

store Casserole can be made 1 day ahead and refrigerated, covered.

potatoes
with cream

PREPARATION TIME 20 MINUTES ▪ COOKING TIME 1 HOUR 15 MINUTES

4 large old potatoes (1.2kg), peeled, sliced thinly
pinch ground nutmeg
1 cup (250ml) cream
¼ cup (20g) grated parmesan cheese
20g butter, chopped coarsely

1 Grease deep 19cm square cake pan; layer potatoes in pan. Sprinkle with nutmeg; pour over cream. Sprinkle with cheese; dot with butter.

2 Bake, covered, in moderate oven 30 minutes. Uncover; bake further 45 minutes or until top is browned and potatoes are tender.

serves 4

per serving 33.3g fat; 2125kJ
store Recipe can be made 1 day ahead and refrigerated, covered.
tip Do not use thickened cream in this recipe.

potato and cauliflower
gratin

PREPARATION TIME 20 MINUTES ■ COOKING TIME 1 HOUR

4 medium carrots (800g), chopped finely

2 eggs

½ cup (125ml) skim milk

½ cup (120g) light sour cream

4 medium potatoes (800g), peeled, chopped coarsely

400g cauliflower, chopped coarsely

4 green onions, chopped finely

1½ cups (100g) fresh white breadcrumbs

2 cloves garlic, crushed

⅔ cup (80g) grated low-fat tasty cheese

1 Boil, steam or microwave carrot until very tender; drain. Blend or process carrot, eggs, milk and sour cream until creamy.

2 Boil, steam or microwave potato and cauliflower, separately, until tender; drain. Combine potato, cauliflower and onion in 2-litre (8-cup) baking dish; pour carrot mixture over top.

3 Combine breadcrumbs, garlic and cheese in small bowl; sprinkle over carrot mixture. *[Can be made 3 hours ahead to this stage and refrigerated, covered.]*

4 Bake, uncovered, in moderately hot oven about 40 minutes, or until heated through and crisp.

serves 6

per serving 16g fat; 1876kJ

tip Pumpkin can be substituted for carrot in this recipe.

mushroom and broccoli
baked spuds

PREPARATION TIME 20 MINUTES ■ COOKING TIME 1 HOUR 20 MINUTES

5 large potatoes (1.2kg)

2 teaspoons vegetable oil

**100g button mushrooms,
  sliced thinly**

85g finely chopped broccoli florets

20g butter

2 tablespoons plain flour

1 cup (250ml) milk

**½ cup (60g) coarsely grated
  cheddar cheese**

1 Scrub potatoes; pierce skin. Place on greased oven tray; bake, uncovered, in moderate oven about 1 hour or until tender. When cool enough to handle, cut 1cm slice off one long side of each potato; scoop out potato flesh, leaving a 5mm shell. Reserve flesh; place shells on oven tray.

2 Heat oil in small saucepan; cook mushrooms and broccoli, stirring, until broccoli is just tender.

3 Heat butter in small saucepan; cook flour, stirring, until mixture is grainy. Remove from heat; gradually stir in milk. Stir over medium heat until sauce boils and thickens. Remove from heat; stir in half of the cheese.

4 Combine potato flesh, mushroom mixture and sauce in large bowl; mix well. Divide potato mixture among potato shells. *[Can be made 1 day ahead to this stage and refrigerated, covered.]*

5 Sprinkle potatoes with remaining cheese. Bake, uncovered, in moderate oven about 10 minutes or until hot.

serves 4

per serving 14.4g fat; 1613kJ

tip Combine potato flesh with one finely chopped green onion and 2 tablespoons each of sour cream and sweet chilli sauce. Divide filling among potato shells and serve topped with extra green onion, sour cream and sweet chilli sauce.

baked tomatoes
with nutty rice filling

PREPARATION TIME 35 MINUTES ▦ COOKING TIME 55 MINUTES

10 medium tomatoes (1.9kg)
2 tablespoons olive oil
1 large brown onion (200g), chopped finely
¼ cup (35g) currants
¼ cup (40g) pine nuts
¾ cup (150g) short-grain rice
1 cup (250ml) water
1 tablespoon coarsely chopped fresh dill
1 tablespoon coarsely chopped fresh thyme
1 tablespoon coarsely chopped fresh parsley

white sauce
30g butter
2½ tablespoons plain flour
1⅓ cups (330ml) milk

1 Cut tops from tomatoes; discard. Spoon pulp, seeds and juice into small bowl; mash. Reserve 1½ cups (375ml) of the pulp mixture.

2 Heat oil in medium frying pan; cook onion, stirring, until soft. Add currants, nuts, rice and the water; simmer, covered with tight-fitting lid, 8 minutes. Remove pan from heat; stir in herbs and reserved pulp mixture.

3 Divide rice mixture among tomatoes, top with white sauce. Place tomatoes in ovenproof dish with enough boiling water to come 1cm up the side of tomatoes.

4 Bake, uncovered, in moderately slow oven about 40 minutes or until tops are browned lightly and tomatoes are heated through.

white sauce Melt butter in medium saucepan. Add flour; stir over heat until mixture is grainy. Remove pan from heat; gradually stir in milk. Stir over heat until mixture boils and thickens; cool slightly.

makes 10

per serving 10.5g fat; 868kJ

chilli and vegetable
frittata

PREPARATION TIME 25 MINUTES ■ COOKING TIME 1 HOUR 15 MINUTES (plus standing time)

2 medium potatoes (400g),
  sliced thinly

1 tablespoon olive oil

1 medium red onion (170g),
  sliced thinly

3 cloves garlic, crushed

1 medium green capsicum (200g),
  sliced thinly

1 medium red capsicum (200g),
  sliced thinly

2 medium red banana chillies,
  sliced thinly

1 green thai chilli, chopped finely

1½ cups (185g) grated
  cheddar cheese

5 eggs, beaten lightly

1 cup (250ml) cream

2 tablespoons finely chopped
  fresh coriander

1 Grease deep 20cm-round cake pan; line base with greaseproof paper.

2 Boil, steam or microwave potato until just tender. Drain; cool.

3 Heat oil in large saucepan; cook onion and garlic, stirring, until onion is soft. Remove from pan.

4 Add capsicums; cook, stirring, until tender. Remove from pan.

5 Add chillies; cook, stirring, until just tender.

6 Layer potato, onion mixture, capsicums and chillies in prepared pan, sprinkling cheese between layers. Pour combined egg, cream and coriander over top. Bake, uncovered, in moderately hot oven 1 hour. Stand in pan 10 minutes before cutting.

serves 4

per serving 54.1g fat; 2750kJ

store Frittata can be made 1 day ahead and refrigerated, covered.

tip Try layering dry chargrilled eggplant and capsicum slices, semi-dried tomatoes, cheese and chopped fresh basil, or make a breakfast frittata with mushrooms, tomato and chives. Ricotta cheese may be substituted for cream to reduce fat and kilojoule count, if preferred.

ricotta and spinach
pasta shells

PREPARATION TIME 20 MINUTES ■ COOKING TIME 1 HOUR 5 MINUTES

32 large pasta shells (280g)

500g spinach

250g low-fat ricotta cheese

500g low-fat cottage cheese

**1½ cups (375ml) tomato
  pasta sauce**

1 cup (250ml) vegetable stock

**1 tablespoon finely grated
  parmesan cheese**

1 Cook pasta in large saucepan of boiling water, uncovered, 3 minutes. Drain; allow to cool slightly.

2 Boil, steam or microwave spinach until just wilted; drain. Squeeze out excess liquid; chop spinach finely. Combine ricotta and cottage cheeses with spinach in medium bowl; mix well. Divide spinach mixture among pasta shells.

3 Combine sauce and stock in 2-litre (8-cup) shallow ovenproof dish. Arrange pasta shells in sauce; sprinkle with parmesan.

4 Bake, covered, in moderate oven about 1 hour or until pasta is tender.

serves 4

per serving 9.7g fat; 2125kJ
store Recipe can be made 1 day ahead and refrigerated, covered.
tip 16 cannelloni shells may be substituted for large pasta shells, if preferred.

double mushroom
sourdough puddings

PREPARATION TIME 25 MINUTES (plus standing time) ▪ COOKING TIME 1 HOUR

500g sourdough bread, cubed

1.125 litres (4½ cups) skim milk

200g swiss brown mushrooms, sliced thinly

150g shiitake mushrooms, sliced thinly

1 clove garlic, crushed

1½ tablespoons finely chopped fresh sage

2 eggs, beaten lightly

2 egg whites

1 Combine bread with 1 cup (250ml) of the milk; refrigerate 15 minutes.

2 Cook mushrooms, garlic and sage in heated medium non-stick saucepan until mushrooms are browned lightly.

3 Divide half of the bread mixture between six 1-cup (250ml) ovenproof moulds. Top with half of the mushroom mixture. Repeat with remaining bread and mushroom mixtures.

4 Combine remaining milk, egg and egg whites in small bowl; whisk until well combined. Divide between moulds; bake, uncovered, in moderate oven about 45 minutes or until firm. Sprinkle with sage, if desired.

serves 6

per serving 4.9g fat; 1215kJ

tip Cover puddings halfway through cooking if the tops are becoming too brown.

olive and sun-dried tomato polenta

PREPARATION TIME 15 MINUTES (plus standing time)
COOKING TIME 35 MINUTES

1 litre (4 cups) vegetable stock
1 cup (170g) polenta
1 cup (200g) coarsely crumbled fetta cheese
2/3 cup (50g) coarsely grated fresh parmesan cheese
1/2 cup firmly packed fresh basil, chopped coarsely
1/3 cup (40g) seeded black olives, halved
2/3 cup (100g) drained sun-dried tomatoes in oil, chopped finely
plain flour
vegetable oil for shallow-frying

1 Lightly grease 20cm-round sandwich cake pan. Bring stock to a boil in large saucepan. Add polenta; simmer, stirring, about 15 minutes or until polenta is very thick.

2 Remove polenta from heat; stir in cheeses, basil, olives and tomato. Press firmly into prepared pan. Cool to room temperature; refrigerate until firm. *[Can be made 1 day ahead to this stage and refrigerated, covered.]*

3 Cut polenta into 16 wedges. Toss polenta in flour; shake away excess. Heat oil in large frying pan. Shallow-fry polenta until browned lightly and crisp both sides; drain on absorbent paper.

serves 8

per serving 31.5g fat; 1759kJ

spiced currant couscous

PREPARATION TIME 20 MINUTES (plus standing time)
COOKING TIME 5 MINUTES

2 teaspoons butter
1 medium brown onion (150g), chopped finely
1 tablespoon garam masala
2 cups (500ml) water
2 cups (400g) couscous
1/2 cup (75g) dried currants

1 Heat butter in medium saucepan; cook onion, stirring, until onion is soft. Add garam masala; cook, stirring, until fragrant. Add the water; bring to a boil. Stir in couscous.

2 Remove from heat; stand, covered, about 5 minutes or until all the water is absorbed. Fluff occasionally, using fork; gently stir in currants.

serves 4

per serving 2.7g fat; 1669kJ

polenta

vegan
PREPARATION TIME 15 MINUTES (plus standing time)
COOKING TIME 35 MINUTES

2 litres (8 cups) water
2 teaspoons salt
2 cups (340g) polenta
½ cup (125ml) olive oil

1 Bring the water and salt to a boil in large saucepan; add polenta. Reduce heat; simmer, stirring about 15 minutes or until polenta is very thick. *[Polenta can be served at this point, piled onto a plate, or continue as below.]*

2 Press mixture into oiled 18cm x 28cm rectangular slice pan. Cool to room temperature; refrigerate until firm*. [Can be made 1 day ahead to this stage and refrigerated, covered.]*

3 Cut polenta into 12 rectangles. Heat oil in large frying pan. Cook polenta until browned lightly and crisp both sides; drain on absorbent paper.

serves 6

per serving 20.1g fat; 1483kJ

couscous tabbouleh

vegan
PREPARATION TIME 20 MINUTES
COOKING TIME 5 MINUTES

2 tablespoons couscous
2 tablespoons boiling water
½ cup finely chopped fresh parsley
1 small tomato (130g), seeded, chopped finely
½ small red onion (50g), chopped finely
1 tablespoon lemon juice
1 teaspoon finely chopped fresh mint

1 Combine couscous and the water in small heatproof bowl. Stir, using fork, until the water is absorbed; cool.

2 Combine couscous, parsley, tomato, onion, juice and mint in large bowl; mix well.

serves 2

per serving 0.3g fat; 346kJ
store Tabbouleh can be made 1 day ahead and refrigerated, covered.

caramelised mixed
onions

PREPARATION TIME 15 MINUTES ■ COOKING TIME 50 MINUTES

1 large bulb garlic (90g)

50g butter

2 tablespoons olive oil

24 golden shallots (290g)

6 spring onions (150g), halved

10 green onions, halved

1 tablespoon balsamic vinegar

1 Separate garlic bulb into cloves; peel cloves. Heat butter and oil in large frying pan; cook garlic, shallots and spring onion about 45 minutes, stirring, until tender and browned.

2 Add green onion; cook, stirring, until just tender. Drizzle with vinegar; serve immediately.

serves 6

per serving 13.5g fat; 619kJ

vegetable accompaniments

International influence comes to life in this diverse selection of Asian and traditional side dishes. Mixed greens with cashews, eggplant crisps and herbed baby potatoes are just a few.

mixed greens
with cashews

PREPARATION TIME 10 MINUTES ■ COOKING TIME 5 MINUTES

vegan

1 tablespoon peanut oil

1 medium brown onion (150g), sliced thinly

1 teaspoon grated fresh ginger

2 cloves garlic, crushed

150g snake beans, cut into 5cm lengths

250g broccoli, chopped coarsely

2 tablespoons vegetable stock

500g choy sum, chopped coarsely

100g snow peas, halved

1 tablespoon black bean sauce

1 tablespoon light soy sauce

½ cup (75g) coarsely chopped cashews, toasted

1 Heat oil in wok or large frying pan; stir-fry onion, ginger and garlic until fragrant. Add beans, broccoli and stock; cook, covered, 2 minutes.

2 Add choy sum, snow peas and sauces; stir-fry until choy sum just wilts. Serve vegetables sprinkled with cashews.

serves 4

per serving 14.8g fat; 909kJ

snake bean
and asparagus salad with citrus dressing

PREPARATION TIME 15 MINUTES ■ COOKING TIME 10 MINUTES

vegan

500g asparagus, trimmed, cut into 6cm lengths

200g snake beans, trimmed, cut into 6cm lengths

2 small tomatoes (260g), chopped finely

1 small red onion (100g), chopped finely

2 cloves garlic, crushed

1 tablespoon lemon juice

2 tablespoons orange juice

1 tablespoon cider vinegar

1 Place asparagus in large saucepan of boiling water. Return to a boil; drain immediately. Refresh in cold water; drain.

2 Place beans in large saucepan of boiling water. Return to a boil; drain immediately. Refresh in cold water; drain.

3 Combine asparagus, beans, tomato and onion in large serving bowl.

4 Combine garlic, juices and vinegar in small jug; pour over salad just before serving.

serves 4

per serving 0.4g fat; 196kJ

eggplant crisps

PREPARATION TIME 15 MINUTES (plus standing time)
COOKING TIME 15 MINUTES

vegan

2 medium eggplants (650g), sliced thinly
coarse cooking salt
oil, for shallow-frying

1 Sprinkle eggplant with salt; stand 15 minutes. Rinse eggplant under cold running water. Drain; pat dry with absorbent paper.

2 Heat oil in large frying pan. Cook eggplant, in batches, over low heat, until browned and crisp; drain on absorbent paper. Crisps can be served warm or cold.

serves 6

per serving 26.4g fat; 1044kJ
store Crisps can be made 2 days ahead and stored in airtight container.

stir-fried greens
with green beans

PREPARATION TIME 10 MINUTES ▓ COOKING TIME 10 MINUTES

vegan

350g green beans, halved

2 tablespoons peanut oil

1 teaspoon sesame oil

2 cloves garlic, crushed

2 teaspoons grated fresh ginger

8 green onions, chopped coarsely

500g spinach, chopped coarsely

670g baby bok choy,
    chopped coarsely

1 tablespoon teriyaki sauce

1 tablespoon salt-reduced
    soy sauce

1 tablespoon mild sweet
    chilli sauce

2 tablespoons finely chopped
    fresh coriander

1 Place beans in large saucepan of boiling water. Return to a boil; drain.

2 Heat oils in wok or large frying pan; stir-fry garlic, ginger and onion until onion is soft.

3 Add beans, spinach and bok choy; stir-fry until bok choy just wilts.

4 Add sauces; stir until hot.

5 Serve sprinkled with coriander.

serves 4

per serving 11.2g fat; 658kJ

herbed baby potatoes

PREPARATION TIME 10 MINUTES ■ COOKING TIME 25 MINUTES

1kg baby new potatoes

1 tablespoon olive oil

60g butter

2 cloves garlic, crushed

2 tablespoons fresh rosemary, chopped finely

1 Place potatoes in large saucepan; cover with cold water. Bring to a boil; remove from heat. Stand in hot water 5 minutes; drain. Let stand until cool enough to handle; cut each potato in half.

2 Heat oil and butter in large frying pan; cook potato, cut-side down, covered, over medium-high heat about 10 minutes or until cut surface is golden and crisp.

3 Add garlic; cook further 5 minutes. Sprinkle rosemary over potato; toss gently.

serves 6

per serving 11.4g fat; 877kJ

potatoes anna

PREPARATION TIME 20 MINUTES ■ COOKING TIME 50 MINUTES

**4 large yellow-fleshed potatoes
(1.2kg), peeled**

100g butter, melted

1 Cut potatoes into very thin slices; pat dry with absorbent paper.

2 Brush butter generously over 23cm-round enamel-coated cast iron pan with sloping sides, or ovenproof pie plate.

3 Place one layer of overlapping potato slices over base of prepared pan; brush with butter. Repeat layering until all slices are used, ending with butter.

4 Bake, covered, in very hot oven 20 minutes. Uncover; bake further 30 minutes or until top is crisp and golden brown and potato is cooked through. Turn onto heatproof plate; cut into wedges. Serve with chervil, if desired.

serves 6

per serving 13.9g fat; 1054kJ

broccolini
with lemon mustard butter

PREPARATION TIME 10 MINUTES ■ COOKING TIME 5 MINUTES

80g soft butter
1 tablespoon seeded mustard
1 tablespoon lemon juice
¼ teaspoon cracked black pepper
600g broccolini

1 Combine butter, mustard, juice and pepper in small bowl. Boil, steam or microwave broccolini until just tender; drain.

2 Just before serving, toss butter mixture through hot broccolini. Serve topped with finely shredded lemon rind, if desired.

serves 8

per serving 6.4g fat; 310kJ
store Butter mixture can be frozen up to 2 months.
tip Broccoli, cut into small florets, can be substituted for broccolini if unavailable.

menus

When you're planning a vegetarian menu, the same rules apply as for a meal containing meat. A balance of flavours, colours and cooking methods is what you're after.

- Don't duplicate flavours and colours – two courses containing tomato or cream is monotonous.
- Don't duplicate cooking methods. A char-grilled first course and a char-grilled main course might be too much of a good thing, although you could get away with it at a barbecue. Two courses containing pastry, however, are definitely too much.
- Make sure you have the right plates and dishes for the meal you're presenting – and enough of them.
- Balance your menu – serve a light first course if the main course is a hearty casserole. Alternatively, fried food such as samosas as a first course need a light fresh dish to follow.
- Do your planning – cook whatever you can in advance and don't include more than one dish that has to be cooked at the last minute – otherwise you'll be tied to the kitchen and you'll never see your guests.
- Since there are no dessert recipes in this book, the dessert suggestions opposite are simple ideas using fresh fruit. By all means serve custards, puddings, pies and ice-creams to give your vegetarian meal a satisfying finish.

al fresco lunch

gazpacho PAGE 34
MAKE 1 DAY AHEAD
add vegetable garnish on serving

onion tart PAGE 79
MAKE 2 DAYS AHEAD

mesclun salad with tarragon dressing PAGE 60
prepare mesclun and dressing 3 hours ahead and toss together just before serving

dessert sprinkle pineapple wedges with sugar, grill and serve sprinkled with fresh mint leaves

low-fat dinner

broad bean and ricotta dip PAGE 12
MAKE 1 DAY AHEAD
serve with crisp vegetable sticks

rigatoni with fetta and herbed tomatoes PAGE 159
serve with warmed crusty Italian bread

snake bean and asparagus salad with citrus dressing PAGE 231

dessert serve slices of fresh melon drizzled with a little green ginger wine

italian feast

marinated olives PAGE 63
MAKE AT LEAST 2 WEEKS AHEAD

roasted capsicums PAGE 62
MAKE 3 DAYS AHEAD

marinated mushrooms PAGE 62
MAKE UP TO 3 MONTHS AHEAD

char-grilled salad with polenta rounds and pesto PAGE 68
PREPARE POLENTA 1 DAY AHEAD

ricotta and spinach pasta shells PAGE 223
MAKE 1 DAY AHEAD
serve with crusty fresh bread

dessert quarter fresh figs, drizzle with muscat and serve with mascarpone

indian banquet

corn and pea samosas PAGE 10
MAKE 1 MONTH AHEAD AND FREEZE

curried eggs PAGE 130
MAKE 1 DAY AHEAD

spinach and pumpkin curry PAGE 168
MAKE 1 DAY AHEAD

spicy vegetables with chickpeas PAGE 204
MAKE 1 DAY AHEAD

serve with steamed rice, or warmed purchased naan and roti

dessert a platter of fresh tropical fruit sprinkled with toasted coconut followed by a small plate of caraway seeds to freshen the breath

cocktail party

mini pappadums with curried egg PAGE 14
MAKE EGG MIXTURE 1 DAY AHEAD

dolmades PAGE 21
MAKE 2 DAYS AHEAD

fetta dip PAGE 17
MAKE 2 DAYS AHEAD
serve with vegetable sticks

cucumber and kumara sushi PAGE 13
MAKE 1 DAY AHEAD

cheese fillo triangles PAGE 16
MAKE 1 MONTH AHEAD AND FREEZE

dessert pass around a large bowl of strawberries with some sifted icing sugar before serving coffee

vegan dinner

tomato and borlotti bean soup PAGE 39
MAKE 2 DAYS AHEAD

Irish soda bread PAGE 45
MAKE 3 HOURS AHEAD

pasta tossed with tofu pesto PAGE 113
MAKE PESTO UP TO 1 WEEK AHEAD

tossed vegetable salad with lemon, garlic and pine nuts PAGE 67
MAKE 3 HOURS AHEAD

dessert poach fresh dates with apples and quinces

glossary

allspice also known as pimento or jamaican pepper; available whole or ground. Tastes like a blend of cinnamon, clove and nutmeg.

artichoke hearts centre of the globe artichoke; sold in cans, or loose in brine.

baking powder a raising agent consisting mainly of two parts cream of tartar to one part bicarbonate of soda (baking soda).

bamboo shoots the shoots of bamboo plants, available in cans.

barley a nutritious grain used in soups and stews as well as whisky- and beer-making. Pearl barley has had the husk discarded and been steamed and polished, much the same as rice.

bean sprouts also called bean shoots. The most common are mung bean, soy bean, alfalfa and snow pea sprouts.

beans
borlotti also known as Roman beans. Pale brown with burgundy markings, they have a smooth texture with a ham-like flavour when cooked.
broad also known as fava beans, these are available fresh, canned and frozen. If fresh, they are best peeled twice, discarding both the outer long green pod and pale-green tough inner shell.
butter also known as lima beans, sold dried and canned. Large beige beans having a mealy texture and mild taste.
cannellini small, dried white bean similar in appearance and flavour to other phaseolus vulgaris: great northern and navy or haricot beans.
Mexe-Beans trade name for a canned pinto bean in chilli sauce mixture. Pinto beans are similar to borlotti beans.
mexican black turtle Latin American and Caribbean small black beans with a tiny white eye, not to be confused with chinese black (soy) beans. Sold dried or canned, great in salsas and soups.
snake long (about 40cm), thin, round green beans, Asian in origin, with a taste similar to string beans and runner beans.
soy extremely nutritious beans that are processed into fresh bean curd and soy milk, as well as fermented products, such as miso and soy sauce. Dried beans can be soaked, then cooked.
vegetarian re-fried pinto beans that are cooked twice; soaked and boiled, then mashed and fried. (Traditionally, the beans are fried in lard but vegetarian versions are available, check the label before purchasing.)

beetroot also known as garden beets, red beets or, simply, beets. A hard, round, sweet root vegetable that is highly nutritious. Eat raw, boiled or roasted.

bicarbonate of soda also known as baking soda.

bok choy also called pak choi or chinese white cabbage. Has a fresh, mild mustard taste and is good braised or in stir-fries. Baby bok choy is tender and more delicate in flavour.

bread
bagels small, ring-shaped bread rolls.
ciabatta in Italian, the word means slipper, which is the traditional shape of this crusty white bread.
lavash flat, unleavened bread of Mediterranean origin.
pitta also known as lebanese bread, this wheat-flour bread is sold in large, flat pieces that separate easily into two paper-thin rounds. Also available in small thick pieces called pitta pocket breads.
sourdough uses a "starter" of fermented flour and water, rather than yeast, giving a slightly sour flavour and chewy texture.

breadcrumbs
fresh fresh bread made into crumbs by grating, blending or processing.
packaged fine-textured, crunchy, purchased white breadcrumbs.
stale one- or two-day-old bread made into crumbs by grating, blending or processing.

broccolini milder and sweeter than traditional broccoli, it is completely edible from flower to stem with a delicate flavour that has a subtle, peppery edge. It is a cross between broccoli and gai lum (chinese broccoli).

burghul also known as bulghur wheat; hulled, steamed wheat kernels that, once dried, are crushed into grains of various sizes. Used in Middle Eastern dishes such as kibbeh and tabbouleh.

buttermilk sold alongside fresh milk products in supermarkets; low-fat milk cultured to give a slightly sour, tangy taste. Low-fat yogurt can be substituted.

cabbage
chinese also known as Peking cabbage or napa cabbage; resembles a cos lettuce in appearance but tastes similar to the common round cabbage. Remove, wash and chop or shred leaves, and braise, steam or stir-fry.
purple has a deep purple-red colour.
savoy loose-leafed, wrinkled variety with bright-green outer leaves.

cajun seasoning used to give an authentic "USA Deep South" spicy cajun flavour to food, this packaged blend of assorted herbs and spices can include paprika, basil, onion, fennel, thyme, cayenne and tarragon.

capers the grey-green buds of a warm climate (usually Mediterranean) shrub, sold either dried and salted or pickled in a vinegar brine; used to enhance sauces and dressings with their piquant flavour.

capsicum also called pepper; discard seeds and membrane before use. Can also be bought char-grilled or sun-dried, in slices, from delicatessens.

caraway a member of the parsley family, available in seed or ground form. Can be used in sweet and savoury dishes.

celeriac tuberous root with brown skin, white flesh and a celery-like flavour.

cheese
cottage fresh, white, unripened curd cheese; we used a low-fat variety.
cream commonly known as "Philly" or "Philadelphia", a soft milk cheese having no less than 33 per cent butterfat.
fetta Greek in origin; a crumbly-textured goat or sheep milk cheese with a sharp, salty taste.
goat made from goat milk, has an earthy, strong taste; available in both soft and firm textures.
gruyere a Swiss cheese having small holes and a nutty, slightly salty flavour.
haloumi a firm, cream-coloured sheep milk cheese matured in brine; somewhat like a minty, salty fetta in flavour, haloumi keeps its shape without melting when briefly grilled or fried.
parmesan a dry, hard cheese made from skim milk or part-skim milk and aged at least a year; the best, from Italy, are called grana or reggiano and are aged for a minimum of three years.
pecorino hard, dry, yellow cheese, which has a sharp pungent taste. Originally from sheep milk, now it is made with cow milk. If unavailable, use parmesan.
ricotta a sweet, fairly moist, fresh curd cheese having a low fat content.
romano a hard, straw-coloured cheese with a grainy texture and sharp, tangy flavour, usually made from a combination of cow and goat or sheep milk; a good grating cheese.
swiss generic name for a variety of cheeses originating in Switzerland, among them emmenthaler and gruyere.

chickpeas also called garbanzos, an irregularly round, sandy-coloured legume used extensively in Mediterranean and Hispanic cooking.

chillies available in different types and sizes. Use rubber gloves when seeding and chopping fresh chillies as they can burn your skin. Removing seeds and membranes lessens the heat level.
banana chillies sweet-flavoured chillies with a long, tapering shape. If they are unavailable, substitute red capsicum.
chilli powder, Mexican a commercial blend of chilli powder, paprika, oregano, cumin, pepper and garlic.
flakes, dried crushed dried chillies.
thai chillies small, medium hot, and bright-red to dark-green in colour.

chinese broccoli also known as gai lum.

chinese rice wine also known as Shao hsing; blended from glutinous rice, millet, yeast and spring water, then aged.

chinese water spinach also known as swamp spinach, long green, ung choy and kang kong; leafy green vegetable available from Asian specialty shops.

chives, garlic have flat leaves and a stronger flavour than chives.

choy sum also known as flowering bok choy or flowering white cabbage.

cinnamon stick dried inner bark of the shoots of the cinnamon tree.

coconut cream the first pressing from grated mature coconut flesh; available in cans and cartons. As a rule, the proportions are four parts coconut to one part water.

coconut milk the second pressing (less rich) from grated mature coconut flesh; available in cans and cartons. A lower-fat type is also sold.

coconut essence concentrated liquid used to give dishes a coconut flavour.

coriander, fresh also known as cilantro or chinese parsley; bright-green herb with a pungent flavour. Often stirred into a dish just before serving for maximum impact. Dried ground coriander is not a suitable substitute.

corn, baby small corn cobs sold fresh or canned in brine.

cornmeal ground dried corn (maize); similar to polenta but slightly coarser. One can be substituted for the other, but textures will vary.

couscous a fine, grain-like cereal product, originally from North Africa; made from semolina.

cucumbers
lebanese also known as european or burpless cucumbers; slender and dark green, favoured for their juiciness and digestibility.
telegraph an old variety dating back to the days when the telegraph was a new invention. Very long and green with ridges running down their entire length; also called continental cucumbers.

currants, dried tiny, almost black raisins, named after a grape variety that originated in Corinth, Greece.

curry paste, thai-style green commercial versions consist of red onion, green chilli, soy bean oil, garlic, galangal, lemon grass, shrimp paste, citrus peel and coriander seeds.

curry powder a blend of ground spices used for convenience when making Indian food. Can consist of some of the following ingredients in varying proportions: dried chilli, cinnamon, coriander, cumin, fennel, fenugreek, mace, cardamom and turmeric. Choose mild or hot to suit your taste and the recipe.

eggplant also known as aubergine. Baby eggplant, known as finger eggplant, are also available. Char-grilled eggplant is available in slices from delicatessens.

fennel also known as finocchio or anise; eaten raw in salads or braised or fried as a vegetable accompaniment. Also the name given to dried seeds having a licorice flavour.

fillo pastry also known as phyllo; tissue-thin pastry sheets purchased chilled or frozen that are easy to work with and very versatile, lending themselves to both sweet and savoury dishes.

flour
buckwheat although not a true cereal, flour is made from its seeds. Available from health food stores.
plain all-purpose flour made from wheat.
wholemeal plain also known as all-purpose wholewheat flour, has no baking powder added.

galangal also known as laos; a dried root that is a member of the ginger family, used whole or ground, having a piquant peppery flavour.

garam masala a blend of spices, originating in North India; based on varying proportions of cardamom, cinnamon, cloves, coriander, fennel and cumin, roasted and ground together. Black pepper and chilli can be added for a hotter version.

garlic salt mixture of fine garlic powder and free-running table salt.

ghee clarified butter, with the milk solids removed; can be heated to a high temperature without burning.

ginger, fresh also known as green or root ginger; the thick, gnarled root of a tropical plant. Can be kept, peeled, covered with dry sherry in a jar and refrigerated, or frozen in an airtight container.

golden shallots also called french shallots, eshalots or, simply, shallots; small, elongated, brown-skinned members of the onion family that grow in tight clusters similar to garlic.

gow gee wrappers wonton wrappers, spring roll or egg pastry sheets can be substituted.

green ginger wine beverage with 14 per cent alcohol which has the taste of fresh ginger. In cooking, substitute dry (white) vermouth if you prefer, or even an equivalent amount of syrup from a jar of preserved ginger.

kaffir lime leaves aromatic leaves of a small citrus tree bearing a wrinkled, yellow-green fruit, originally grown in South Africa and South-East Asia. Used fresh or dried in many Asian dishes.

kumara Polynesian name of orange-fleshed sweet potato often confused with yam.

lemon grass a tall, clumping, lemon-smelling and tasting, sharp-edged grass; the white lower part of each stem is chopped and used in Asian cooking.

lettuces
iceberg a heavy, firm, round lettuce with tightly packed leaves and crisp texture.
lamb's also known as lamb's tongue, corn salad or mâche, it has clusters of tiny, tender, nutty-tasting leaves.

mesclun a salad mix that consists of an assortment of young lettuce and other green leaves, including baby spinach leaves, mizuna and curly endive.
mignonette deep-red or bright-green tinged with red; firm, crisp leaves with a slightly bitter taste.
oak leaf also known as Feville de Chene. Available in red and green leaf.
radicchio an Italian lettuce with dark burgundy leaves and a bitter taste.

macadamia nuts rich and buttery nuts native to Australia. Store in refrigerator because of their high oil content.

miso paste is grouped into two main categories – red and white, although the "red" is dark brown in colour and the "white" is more the colour of weak tea. Made in Japan, miso is a paste made from cooked, mashed, salted and fermented soy beans, and it is a common ingredient in soups, sauces and dressings. Also known as misi.

mushrooms
button small, cultivated white mushrooms having a delicate, subtle flavour.
cap slightly larger, opened mushrooms with a flavour stronger than buttons.
cloud ear also known as wood ear or dried black fungus; swells to about five times its dried size when soaked.
flat large, soft, flat mushrooms with a rich, earthy flavour, sometimes misnamed field mushrooms.
oyster also known as abalone; grey-white mushroom shaped like a fan.
shiitake also called chinese black mushrooms; used mainly in Chinese and Japanese cooking.
straw cultivated Chinese mushroom with an earthy flavour; sold canned in brine.
swiss brown light- to dark-brown mushrooms with full-bodied flavour. Button or cap mushrooms can be substituted.

mustard
dijon mustard pale-brown, distinctly flavoured, fairly mild French mustard.
mustard seeds black mustard seeds are also known as brown mustard seeds and are more pungent than the white

lamb's lettuce

rocket

(or yellow) seeds that are used in most prepared mustards.

seeded mustard also known as wholegrain, this French-style coarse-grain mustard is made from crushed mustard seeds and Dijon-style French mustard.

noodles

fried crispy egg noodles that are packaged (commonly a 100g packet) and are already deep-fried.

rice stick dried noodles, available flat and wide or very thin; made from rice flour and water.

somen very thin, dried wheat noodles from Japan; sometimes made with egg and then called tamago somen.

thin/thick fresh egg made from wheat flour and eggs; vary in thickness from fine strands to pieces as thick as a shoelace.

nori a type of dried seaweed used in Japanese cooking as a flavouring, garnish or for sushi. Sold in thin sheets.

oil

chilli made by steeping red chillies in vegetable oil, intensely hot in flavour.

cooking-oil spray vegetable oil in an aerosol can, available in supermarkets.

olive made from the pressing of tree-ripened olives. Especially good for everyday cooking and as an ingredient. Extra virgin and virgin are the best, while extra light or light refers to taste, not fat levels.

peanut pressed from ground peanuts; most commonly used in Asian cooking because of its high smoke point.

sesame made from roasted, crushed white sesame seeds; a flavouring rather than a cooking medium.

olive paste made from olives, olive oil, salt, vinegar and herbs.

olives

green have a tart taste and come from fruit picked before it is fully mature.

kalamata almond-shaped, dark-purple Greek olives soaked in a wine vinegar marinade. Sold in olive oil or vinegar.

ligurian very small, purple-black and sweeter than most other olives; excellent in salads and pasta dishes.

onions

fried, bottled commercially deep-fried onions available from Asian food stores.

green also known as scallion or (incorrectly) shallot; an immature onion picked before the bulb has formed, having a long, bright-green edible stalk.

red also known as spanish, red spanish or bermuda onion; a sweet-flavoured, large, purple-red onion.

spring have crisp, narrow, green-leafed tops and a fairly large, sweet white bulb.

pappadums sun-dried wafers made from a combination of lentil and rice flours, oil and spices.

paprika ground dried red capsicum (pepper), available sweet and hot.

parsley, flat-leaf also known as continental or italian parsley.

parsnips long, tapering white root vegetables with sweet, herb-like flavour.

pasta sauce, bottled a prepared tomato-based sauce (sometimes called ragu or sugo on the label); have varying degrees of thickness and kinds of spicing.

pecans native to the United States and now grown locally; golden-brown, buttery and rich. Good in savoury as well as sweet dishes; especially good in salads.

pepitas dried pumpkin seeds.

pepper, seasoned a packaged preparation of black pepper, red capsicum, paprika and garlic.

pine nuts also known as pignoli; small, cream-coloured kernels taken from the cones of different varieties of pine trees.

pistachios pale-green, delicately flavoured nuts inside hard, off-white shells. To peel, soak shelled nuts in boiling water for about 5 minutes; drain, then pat dry with absorbent paper. Rub skin with cloth to peel.

polenta a flour-like cereal made of ground corn (maize); similar to cornmeal but finer and lighter in colour; also the name of the dish made from it.

potatoes, yellow-fleshed use varieties such as desiree, bintje, nicola and spunta.

pumpkin, jap also called Hokkaido. Large, glossy, dark-green skin with pale-yellow speckles and deep-yellow flesh; has a pleasant sweet flavour.

rice

arborio small, round-grain rice that is well suited to absorb a large amount of liquid; especially suited to risotto.

basmati a white, fragrant long-grained rice. It should be washed several times before cooking.

brown natural whole grain.

calrose a medium-sized grain that is extremely versatile; can be used instead of both long- and short-grain varieties.

wild rice not a true member of the rice family, wild rice is from North America. It is expensive as it is difficult to cultivate but has a distinctive flavour. A wild rice/brown rice blend is also available.

rice paper mostly from Vietnam (banh trang). Made from rice paste and stamped into rounds, with a woven pattern. Stores well at room temperature. The sheets are quite brittle and will break if dropped, but when dipped momentarily in water they become pliable wrappers for fried food and for eating fresh (uncooked) vegetables.

rigani, dried wild oregano, native to Greece, that is an integral part of a traditional Greek salad. Replace with dried oregano if unavailable.

rigatoni large, grooved macaroni that traps sauce in its grooves and hollows.

rocket also known as arugula, rugola and rucola; a peppery-tasting green leaf which can be used similarly to baby spinach – eaten raw in salads or cooked in soups, risotto and the like.

saffron stigma of a member of the crocus family, available in strands or ground form; imparts a yellow-orange colour to food once infused. Quality varies greatly; the best is the most expensive spice in the world. Should be stored in the freezer.

sake Japan's favourite rice wine, sake is used in cooking, marinading and as part of dipping sauces. If sake is unavailable, dry sherry, vermouth or brandy can be used as a substitute. When consumed as a drink, it is served warm; to do this, stand the container in hot water about 20 minutes to warm the sake.

salt, rock mined salt that comes in different grades, usually quite coarse.

sambal oelek (also ulek or olek): Indonesian in origin; a salty paste made from chillies, garlic and ginger.

sauces

black bean a Chinese sauce made from fermented soy beans, spices, water and wheat flour.

chilli sauce, sweet a comparatively mild, Thai-style sauce made from red chillies, sugar, garlic and vinegar.

chinese barbecue sauce a thick, sweet and salty commercial sauce used in marinades; made from fermented soy beans, vinegar, garlic, pepper and various spices. Available from Asian specialty stores.

fish sauce also named nam pla or nuoc nam; made from pulverised salted fermented fish, most often anchovies. Has a pungent smell and strong taste.

hoisin sauce a thick, sweet and spicy Chinese paste made from salted fermented soy beans, onions and garlic.

oyster sauce Asian in origin, this rich, brown sauce is made from oysters and their brine, cooked with salt and soy sauce, and thickened with starches. Vegetarian mushroom oyster sauce is available from Asian food stores.

pizza sauce made from tomatoes, salt, herbs and spices; sold in small tubs to be spread over pizza bases.

plum sauce a thick, sweet and sour dipping sauce made from plums, vinegar, sugar, chillies and spices.

satay sauce traditional Indonesian/ Malaysian spicy peanut sauce served with grilled meat skewers. Make your

tat soi

own or buy one of the many packaged versions available from supermarkets or specialty Asian food stores.

soy sauce made from fermented soy beans. Several varieties are available in most supermarkets and Asian food stores. Light soy sauce is, as the name suggests, light in colour; it is generally quite salty. Thick, sweet soy sauce is less salty and is darker due to longer brewing and the addition of molasses.

Tabasco sauce brand name of an extremely fiery sauce made from vinegar, hot red peppers and salt.

teriyaki sauce a homemade or commercially bottled sauce usually made from soy sauce, mirin, sugar, ginger and other spices; it imparts a distinctive glaze when brushed on grilled meat.

sesame seeds tiny oval seeds harvested from the tropical plant Seasamum indicum; a good source of calcium. To toast: spread evenly on tray, toast in moderate oven briefly. Black and white are the most common, however there are also red and brown varieties.

shrimp paste also known as trasi and blanchan; a strong-scented, almost solid preserved paste made of salted dried shrimp. Pungent flavouring used in many South-East Asian soups and sauces.

sichuan hot bean paste a paste made of fermented soy beans, especially popular in Sichuan cooking; the heat is from the addition of chilli. Other flavourings, such as garlic, sesame oil and sugar are sometimes added.

silverbeet also known as swiss chard and mistakenly called spinach; a member of the beet family grown for its tasty green leaves and celery-like stems. Best cooked rather than eaten raw.

snow peas also called mange tout ("eat all"). Snow pea tendrils, the growing shoots of the plant, are also sold by greengrocers.

spinach also known as english spinach and, incorrectly, silverbeet. Tender green leaves are good uncooked in salads or added to soups, stir-fries and stews just before serving.

sugar we used coarse, granulated table sugar, also known as crystal sugar, unless otherwise specified.

palm sugar also known as jaggery, jawa and gula melaka; from the coconut palm. Dark-brown to black in colour and usually sold in rock-hard cakes. The sugar of choice in Indian and most of the South-East Asian cooking.

raw sugar natural brown granulated sugar.

sunflower seed kernels from dried, husked sunflower seeds.

swede a type of turnip which is also known as rutabaga.

taco seasoning a packaged seasoning mix meant to duplicate the Mexican sauce made of oregano, cumin, chillies and various other spices.

tahini a rich, sesame-seed paste, similar to peanut butter in consistency; used in most Middle Eastern cuisines, especially Lebanese, in dips and sauces.

tamari a thick, dark soy sauce made mainly from soy beans, without the wheat (used in standard soy sauces). It is used in dishes where the flavour of soy is important, such as dipping sauces or marinades.

tat soi also known as rosette pak choy, tai gu choy, chinese flat cabbage; a tender variety of bok choy developed to grow close to the ground so it is easily protected from frost.

tempeh produced by a natural culture of soy beans; has a chunky, chewy texture.

tofu also known as bean curd; this off-white, custard-like product is made similarly to cheese, but from soy bean "milk". A good source of protein, it comes fresh as soft or firm and is available from the refrigerated section in supermarkets and Asian food stores. Fried tofu, small cubes of tofu already deep-fried, can be purchased ready for use, as can pressed dried sheets of tofu. Leftover fresh tofu can be refrigerated in water (which is changed daily) for up to 4 days. Silken tofu refers to the method by which it is made – where it is strained through silk.

tomato paste triple-concentrated tomato puree used to flavour soups, stews, sauces and casseroles.

tomatoes
canned whole peeled tomatoes in natural juices.

egg also called plum or Roma, these are smallish, oval-shaped tomatoes much used in Italian cooking and salads.

sun-dried (dehydrated tomatoes); we used sun-dried tomatoes packaged in oil, unless otherwise specified.

vegetarian bacon a vegan version of bacon made from processed gluten.

vietnamese mint not a mint at all, this narrow-leafed pungent herb, also known as cambodian leaf and laksa leaf (daun laks), is widely used in many Asian soups and salads.

vine leaves we used vine leaves in brine; available in jars and packets.

vinegars
balsamic authentic only from the province of Modena, Italy; made from a regional wine of white trebbiano grapes specially processed and then aged in antique wooden casks to give the exquisite pungent flavour.

cider made from fermented apple juice.

raspberry made from fresh raspberries steeped in a white wine vinegar.

red wine based on fermented red wine.

rice based on fermented rice, colourless and flavoured with sugar and salt. Also known as seasoned rice vinegar.

rice wine made from fermented rice.

sherry natural vinegar that is aged in oak according to the traditional Spanish system.

tarragon white wine vinegar infused with fresh tarragon.

water chestnuts resemble chestnuts in appearance, hence the English name. They are small brown tubes with a crisp, white, nutty-tasting flesh. Their crunchy texture is best experienced fresh, however, canned water chestnuts are more easily obtained and can be kept about a month, once opened, under refrigeration.

watercress member of the mustard family; small, crisp, deep-green rounded leaves with a slightly bitter, peppery flavour. Good in salads, soups and sandwiches.

yeast a 7g ($^1/_4$oz) sachet of dried yeast (2 teaspoons) is equal to 15g ($^1/_2$oz) compressed yeast if substituting one for the other.

yellow split peas (toor dhal) also known as field peas, this legume is suitable for purees, dhals and soups.

zucchini also known as courgette; green, yellow or grey member of the squash family having edible flowers.

watercress

index

facts and figures

Wherever you live, you'll be able to use our recipes with the help of these easy-to-follow conversions. While these conversions are approximate only, the difference between an exact and the approximate conversion of various liquid and dry measures is but minimal and will not affect your cooking results.

dry measures

metric	imperial
15g	1/2oz
30g	1oz
60g	2oz
90g	3oz
125g	4oz (1/4lb)
155g	5oz
185g	6oz
220g	7oz
250g	8oz (1/2lb)
280g	9oz
315g	10oz
345g	11oz
375g	12oz (3/4lb)
410g	13oz
440g	14oz
470g	15oz
500g	16oz (1lb)
750g	24oz (11/2lb)
1kg	32oz (2lb)

liquid measures

metric	imperial
30ml	1 fluid oz
60ml	2 fluid oz
100ml	3 fluid oz
125ml	4 fluid oz
150ml	5 fluid oz (1/4 pint/1 gill)
190ml	6 fluid oz
250ml	8 fluid oz
300ml	10 fluid oz (1/2 pint)
500ml	16 fluid oz
600ml	20 fluid oz (1 pint)
1000ml (1 litre)	13/4 pints

helpful measures

metric	imperial
3mm	1/8in
6mm	1/4in
1cm	1/2in
2cm	3/4in
2.5cm	1in
5cm	2in
6cm	21/2in
8cm	3in
10cm	4in
13cm	5in
15cm	6in
18cm	7in
20cm	8in
23cm	9in
25cm	10in
28cm	11in
30cm	12in (1ft)

helpful measures

The difference between one country's measuring cups and another's is, at most, within a 2 or 3 teaspoon variance. (For the record, 1 Australian metric measuring cup holds approximately 250ml.) The most accurate way of measuring dry ingredients is to weigh them. When measuring liquids, use a clear glass or plastic jug with the metric markings. (One Australian metric tablespoon holds 20ml; one Australian metric teaspoon holds 5ml.)

Note: North America, NZ and the UK use 15ml tablespoons. All cup and spoon measurements are level.

We use large eggs having an average weight of 60g.

how to measure

When using graduated metric measuring cups, shake dry ingredients loosely into the appropriate cup. Do not tap the cup on a bench or tightly pack the ingredients unless directed to do so. Level top of measuring cups and measuring spoons with a knife. When measuring liquids, place a clear glass or plastic jug with metric markings on a flat surface to check accuracy at eye level.

oven temperatures

These oven temperatures are only a guide. Always check the manufacturer's manual.

	°C (Celsius)	°F (Fahrenheit)	Gas Mark
Very slow	120	250	1
Slow	150	300	2
Moderately slow	160	325	3
Moderate	180 - 190	350 - 375	4
Moderately hot	200 - 210	400 - 425	5
Hot	220 - 230	450 - 475	6
Very hot	240 - 250	500 - 525	7

Editor *Debbie Quick*
Designer *Alison Windmill*
Project editor (food) *Karen Green*

Test Kitchen Staff
Food editor *Pamela Clark*
Associate food editor *Karen Hammial*
Assistant food editors *Kirsty McKenzie, Louise Patniotis*
Home economists *Clare Bradford, Emma Braz,*
Kimberley Coverdale, Kelly Cruickshanks,
Sarah Hobbs, Amanda Kelly, Alison Webb
Test kitchen manager *Elizabeth Hooper*
Editorial co-ordinator *Juliet Ingersoll*
Stylists *Clare Bradford, Carolyn Fienberg,*
Kay Francis, Jane Hann, Cherise Koch, Vicki Liley,
Michelle Noerianto, Sarah O'Brien
Photographers *Scott Cameron, Robert Clark, Robert Taylor*

Home Library Staff
Editor-in-chief *Mary Coleman*
Managing editor *Susan Tomnay*
Senior writer and editor *Georgina Bitcon*
Senior editor *Liz Neate*
Chief sub-editor *Julie Collard*
Sub-editor *Debbie Quick*
Art director *Michele Withers*
Designers *Mary Keep, Caryl Wiggins, Alison Windmill*
Studio manager *Caryl Wiggins*
Editorial coordinator *Fiona Lambrou*
Editorial assistant *Natalie Liechte*
Book sales manager *Jennifer McDonald*

Chief executive officer *John Alexander*
Group publisher *Jill Baker*
Publisher *Sue Wannan*

Produced by *The Australian Women's Weekly*
Home Library, Sydney.
Colour separations by ACP Colour Graphics Pty Ltd,
Sydney. Printing by Toppan in Hong Kong.
Published by ACP Publishing Pty Limited,
54 Park St, Sydney; GPO Box 4088, Sydney, NSW 1028.
Ph: (02) 9282 8618 Fax: (02) 9267 9438.
awwhomelib@acp.com.au
www.awwbooks.com.au

AUSTRALIA: Distributed by Network Distribution
Company, GPO Box 4088, Sydney, NSW 1028.
Ph: (02) 9282 8777 Fax: (02) 9264 3278.
UNITED KINGDOM: Distributed by Australian
Consolidated Press (UK), Moulton Park Business Centre,
Red House Rd, Moulton Park, Northampton, NN3 6AQ
Ph: (01604) 497 531 Fax: (01604) 497 533
acpukltd@aol.com
CANADA: Distributed by Whitecap Books Ltd, 351 Lynn Ave,
North Vancouver, BC, V7J 2C4, Ph: (604) 980 9852.
NEW ZEALAND: Distributed by Netlink Distribution
Company, Level 4, 23 Hargreaves St, College Hill,
Auckland 1, Ph: (9) 302 7616.
SOUTH AFRICA: Distributed by PSD Promotions (Pty) Ltd,
PO Box 1175, Isando 1600, SA, Ph: (011) 392 6065, and
CNA Limited, Newsstand Division, PO Box 10799,
Johannesburg 2000, SA, Ph: (011) 491 7500.

The great vegetarian cookbook.
Includes index.
ISBN 1 86396 228 X

1. Vegetarian cookery. I. Title: Australian Women's Weekly.
(Series: Australian Women's Weekly Home Library).
641.5636

© ACP Publishing Pty Limited 2001
ABN 18 053 273 546

This publication is copyright. No part of it may be
reproduced or transmitted in any form without the
written permission of the publishers.

Photographers: *Kevin Brown, Robert Clark, Paul Clark,*
Justine Kerrigan, Andre Martin, Georgia Moxham, Robert Taylor,
Ashley Mackevicius, Joe Filshie, Scott Cameron, Jon Waddy,
Alan Benson, Rowan Fotheringham, Louise Lister, Valerie Martin,
Gerry Colley, Rob Shaw, Rosemary Ingram, Russell Brooks.

Stylists: *Jon Allen, Rosemary de Santis, Carolyn Fienberg,*
Jacqui Hing, Cherise Koch, Sarah O'Brien, Anna Phillips,
Jenny Wells, Kay Francis, Michelle Noerianto, Trish Heagerty,
Marie-Helene Clauzon, Jane Hann, Lucy Andrews, Vicki Liley,
Georgina Dolling, Clare Bradford, Sophia Young, Wendy Berecry,
Lisa Martin, Paul Clark, Janet Mitchell, Katy Holder, Lucy Kelly.

Cover: Char-grilled salad with polenta rounds and pesto, page 68
Photographer: Ian Wallace
Stylist: Sarah O'Brien

Back cover: Mushroom and leek tarts, page 84
Photographer: Susie Ferris
Stylist: Sarah O'Brien